T0113915

FROM HIS HEART TO YOURS

PAM CLOONAN

WestBow
P R E S S®
A DIVISION OF THOMAS NELSON
& ZONDERVAN

Copyright © 2022 Pam Cloonan.

All rights reserved. No part of this book may be used or reproduced by any means,
graphic, electronic, or mechanical, including photocopying, recording, taping or by
any information storage retrieval system without the written permission of the author
except in the case of brief quotations embodied in critical articles and reviews.

This book is a work of non-fiction. Unless otherwise noted, the author and the publisher
make no explicit guarantees as to the accuracy of the information contained in this book
and in some cases, names of people and places have been altered to protect their privacy.

You are free to copy all or part of this book if it is to spiritually benefit those you give it to.

WestBow Press
A Division of Thomas Nelson & Zondervan
1663 Liberty Drive
Bloomington, IN 47403
www.westbowpress.com
844-714-3454

Because of the dynamic nature of the Internet, any web addresses or links contained in
this book may have changed since publication and may no longer be valid. The views
expressed in this work are solely those of the author and do not necessarily reflect the
views of the publisher, and the publisher hereby disclaims any responsibility for them.

Any people depicted in stock imagery provided by Getty Images are models,
and such images are being used for illustrative purposes only.
Certain stock imagery © Getty Images.

Scripture quotations taken from The Holy Bible, New International
Version® NIV® Copyright © 1973 1978 1984 2011 by Biblica, Inc.
TM. Used by permission. All rights reserved worldwide.

ISBN: 978-1-6642-5635-4 (sc)
ISBN: 978-1-6642-5637-8 (hc)
ISBN: 978-1-6642-5636-1 (e)

Library of Congress Control Number: 2022901793

WestBow Press rev. date: 06/10/2022

INTRODUCTION

After 47 years of leaning into God and learning to hear His voice, He has challenged me to be silent. Ecclesiastes 5:1(NIV) hit me like a blast of thunder: "Guard your steps when you go to the house of God. Draw near to LISTEN..." I am almost speechless at how He has opened the way to receive His wisdom and directions each morning as I sit before Him.

I praise and worship Him as I pray and imagine making my way through the Spirit of the Tabernacle, being aware that Jesus is the Sacrifice, the Cleanser, the Light of the World, the Bread of Life, the Intercessor, and God. He has forgiven, cleansed, and led me through communion with Him to the entrance of the Holy of Holies, where I stand silent and enter His Presence.

He begins to speak, as I am sure He has spoken to you...with a picture, a word, a concept...but He doesn't expand on it until I start to write down what I see or sense.

These words have become a great source of comfort and edification both to me and to those who have read them—hence, this book. I have been greatly encouraged to publish them and as one friend put it, "So I can have them at my fingertips all the time."

I pray that you will be touched in the same way as you read the Father's words from His Heart to Yours in a deeply personal way.

THE POWER OF THE FATHER'S HEART

THE LOVE OF the Father. Who can know it? An earthly father has tasted and shared only a small imitation of it.

Imagine forming your child from its very inception. You fill every touch with a love so strong no one on earth can understand or experience it. Every part of this child's body, mind and spirit is formed to receive love. It is encased with a promise of what it is to be. Then you give birth to it with the joy of watching it grow into the fullness of what you have made.

But then—an excruciating pain—a wicked attack! The move against this child to rob, kill and destroy its life and purpose. There is no power on earth strong enough to save it, for it comes by its own choice. It is marred and depleted, its vision and hope fade, for the fear it carries from the attack constantly whispers that it will come again. And so it is best not to try, but to succumb to a lesser life, a lesser plan, and just survive its years until the end. As the dreams and visions fade, passing time assures they will not return.

But then! The Father rises, and in His power, He sends a Savior! The Savior, Who by His own blood, washes the child, cleansing it of its wounds and sin. A new life is born, and its vision is not only restored but empowered.

The Father's heart is filled with tears of happiness in this restored life that has filled His creation. For every cell still carries the plan—its strength is increased, and the Spirit of God will be its armor.

"This is My plan for all I have created—this is why My love must be your greatest weapon. Deliver My love to all you know, and you will be filled continually with the love you share. The more you share My heart, the greater your heart will be."

THE BIBLE'S HEARTBEAT

IN MY PRAYER time this morning, I was lead—almost magnetically pulled—to just place my hand on the Bible. Just to rest it there. With that came a love for its written word that just flowed into me at a level deeper than I have ever known. I realized it wasn't my love for the Bible I was feeling but the full context of His love poured out on its pages. I have been asking the Lord to help me understand how it, His Word, is actually alive—how it is health and medicine to our bodies. How does that work?

Then I felt, almost like a heartbeat, how He had poured His own love, life, and goodness into His Word—with an ache to express the depth of His love.

I know for myself, sometimes I read it or just study it. But other times I read it with my heart trying to climb inside His heart so to speak. That's when it becomes an experience. So I sit here looking at the Bible—closed, clearly exposing hundreds of pages all filled with His heart. It is almost like touching His Presence—the depth of His being. It's right here in front of me. He reaches out to us, calls us, and gives us His life, revealing His deep desire to have us to Himself forever. And so, the words come off the pages, go into our hearts, and give us life.

Of all the beautiful and incredible things we find in creation, to me this is the most amazing, tangible experience of God.

"The Word gave life to everything that was created and His life brought light to everyone." (John 1:4-5 NLT)

TREMBLE

AND SO, HE begins to speak:

"Listen and tremble. I am the source of all power. It is My power that holds up the universe. The only thing in the world that can move Me is the sincerity of your tears.

I melt with love for you. When your prayers are poured out for others, for righteousness, for love and restoration, for My glory, it can cause Me to tremble with a love that moves Me to act in harmony with your heart. You tremble with fear, but I tremble with love.

A righteous prayer is the energy that moves us as one. It is not you, it is not Me, but it is the power of our unity by your humble agreement with My heart. For I yearn for you to seek My will and My heart in sincere hunger. It is this submissive agreement that causes My heart to overflow. It is not your plea that causes Me to move but the sweet surrender to the goodness of My will.

Prayer is not asking, prayer is coming into agreement with Me and My will for man. So don't hesitate or strain. If your prayer is in righteousness, it is not of you, it is of Me. You have only to agree. This is faith. This is where faith is born."

A NEW BAPTISM

"JUST AS IN rising out of the water of Baptism, you were raised to new life in Jesus, just as the baptism in My Holy Spirit brought revelation and power, so now a baptism is coming that will bring a greater revelation of Me than has ever been seen or known.

This will come by love, not by straining or imploring, but by love. It will be poured out without measure to all who are willing to lay their lives down and receive it. Love is a light in the darkness. So with that love, you will see in a new light. This light will illuminate the core of all existence, the core of creation, the core of man, and the core of eternity.

My love poured out in this Baptism will bring light to the darkness and healing to the wings of restoration. Why do I tell you not to judge? Your judgment only brings more darkness. Be aware that judgment is not the same as correction. Correction comes from love, bringing light and understanding. Kindness is a door that always opens a heart, for it is moved by love. The heart is hungry for it and will always receive kindness. This is the beginning of the outpouring, so get out of self and seek to be My Hand and My voice. This love is the most powerful tool I have given you. Pray for it."

AN EMPTY HOSE

"A HOSE HAS no power on its own. It stays where it is put and is of no use. But when the power is turned on, it is filled with the water that brings life to all it touches. It is not the hose that brings the blessing, it is what it contains that carries the power, and all it touches will bloom and become what it was intended to be.

Man is like that hose—unless he is filled with My water, he is useless in the Kingdom of God. I give you the Living Water, and it will be a never-ending flow within you. Just as you can increase the amount of water flowing out of the hose, you can increase the flow of My Living Water. Just fill yourself with My Word, and seek the increase of My Holy Spirit within you.

Don't settle and stay in one place, but continually seek more of Me through My Holy Spirit. Don't ever be satisfied, pray for the flow of water to increase both in measure and in power. In this, you will grow more and more intimate with Me, and your purpose in the Kingdom will develop into an eternal ministry.

Don't be an observer, be empowered. Ask Me earnestly to increase the flow, and the size of your 'garden' will spread continually.

Bring the answer to those who thirst and they will blossom without end. Then, what joy will be in your heart as you look out at the fruit of your labor. And what joy will fill My heart as I look upon you."

THE CONTENT OF TIME

"TIME. IT IS a measure that limits you in whatever you are doing. So treasure it like a treasured jewel. Not using time wisely is like having a jewel but keeping it under lock and key. Use your time. Display it by having something worthwhile to show for it.

What better use than to be with Me or to be about My business. Use your gifts in this time—minister to the needy, touch a heart, give a helping hand, do your job, help someone do theirs, share My love, and quietly 'be' My love to someone.

Take time to rest, but not alone, rest in Me. I have made you to be useful, so use the fullness of who you are. This is where the devil comes as a thief, if he can steal your time, he can steal your use.

Don't waste who you are."

MY WORK

"SPEAK WORDS OF love, be kind, speak truth, do not compromise. Listen, heal, anoint, and pray for others to spread the Good News.

Know that I am with you, I will use you and work through you. Never step backward only move forward, but in unity with Me.

As you walk, concentrate on the unseen that you might call it into being. Concentrate on the unsaved and bring them to Me. Concentrate on the poor, the rich, the lonely that need to be filled with My Presence. See My Kingdom coming as you move, for daily, I invade your world through My servants. Have no fear, trust Me and go…"

YOU SPEAK—I TOUCH

"YOU KNOW NOT what you touch when you touch Me with your earnest prayer. You open the flow of power and love to move toward you and those you minister to.

Be aware of MY Love and allow it to be active in you. It is not a fantasy or an attraction that would fill a moment or a period of time. My love is the power to speak, embrace, bless, and bring My Presence. It is a vehicle to others' hearts, a means I can use to touch them and bring the truth of My Presence into their lives.

When you move in My love, you move in an intangible power, like the wind or even a breeze. It will have its effect depending on the strength of its 'wind.' Do not be afraid to express it. The world contains so many tangible pleasures that feed the flesh, that love seems to have lost its power.

Pray hard for others and let My love for them fill you. Then bring the world back to My love."

THE MELODY OF TRUTH

"MY PLEASURE IS in My people who yearn to hear My voice, who want to know and understand My will.

Give Me your ears as you come before Me.

Give me your heart, and then listen to its song.

Music is not just found in melody but in the harmony of truth. And truth is 'music' to your spiritual ears. My voice gave and gives life to My creation, so all creation sings My praise. When you find yourself awestruck at the beauty in this world, what you are feeling inside is the indescribable melody of life, the truth of My existence and power.

Blessed are they who hear this sound, who know My voice and 'sing' with My creation.

My abundance overflows in your heart because in this, you are one with Me and all I have made.

Take time to share in this union, to worship with its wonder. 'All creation groans for the manifestation of the sons of God.' (Romans 8:19 ESV) Hear its cry and feed it My praise."

LOVING THROUGH YOU

"HONOR OTHERS WITH your words. Allow Me to make you a blessing by being willing to see the good and speak it out. Seek Me as you go and be confident I will use you. Lift up your eyes, look for the need, and be willing to fill it. I want to love through you. This is My ardent desire. How else will the world come to know My love for them?

Come early to listen, to be filled and carry that fullness with you throughout the day. The more you pour out, the greater your fullness will be. Look and live to love. Think of the person you like and respect the least—you are alone with them. What would your words be? As you leave, what seeds have you planted? Would they have been touched by My goodness?

It's easy to love the lovely. But, 'I am sending you out among wolves.' (Matthew 10:16 AMP) Are you willing?"

YOUR HARVEST

"COME INTO MY Kingdom. Bring with you all you have accumulated by your gifts and ministry. Be filled with the grain of harvest, the fruit of your labors. My angels shall help you to carry it all. You may be surprised at the fullness of what you bring. When you live normal, natural lives but exhibit My fruit, you will have a harvest.

Each time you extend yourself to another, there will be a harvest. Whether you gave birth to its beginning, fed it on its way, or reaped the blessed results, it is your harvest.

Be aware of the importance of your contribution. Many think because they haven't reaped, the sowing doesn't count. But I say, it all counts. Can a house exist without the hidden foundation? Every step in growth is equally important, otherwise, there would be no finished work. It is not just the finisher who gets the reward, but the entire team.

So as you live your life, planting seeds of love, healing, kindness, and understanding, let joy be free in your heart, knowing you have done your job."

TRUST AND REST IN ME

"COME TO MY table. Come and share a meal with Me. Drink until you are full of life and energy. Have no fear for there is no end to My supply. I have come to comfort you, to hold your hand and to heal your heart. What are your worries? What pressure is in your heart? Who are you concerned for? Be at rest. Do you not think I know these things and share your burden?

Rest. Joy only comes through confident faith, anything less is of the thief. I am your Father and your Creator. Give Me your cares and let them go."

MY TIMELESS SPIRIT

"TIME. THE BARRIER. The limit. The exercise of arranging it to meet all needs and responsibilities. It is a hard task master. Schedules. Lists. Jobs. They are the rulers of your life.

Where do I fit into that schedule of yours? Take your time alone with Me. But when you do, do you pray with your mind as if it's a part of your responsibilities, or do you pray by the Holy Spirit? When you join your spirit to Mine in your heart, you are free to be there as you go through the rest of your day. If you stay conscious of My Presence and voice within you, I will guide you through all you do and give you grace and anointing to leave a blessing in every work.

There is simply a oneness in love that will touch all you do. As you move into your day, I do not leave. I walk with you. Learn in Me that there is no time. Let your body and soul do its work, but let Me do it with you in a conscious anointed way. Enjoy My presence and pleasure in sharing all of your life. I don't want a section of your life—I want all of it."

THE LESSER LIGHTS

"HAVE YOU NOTICED the different lights in your world? One so bright for the day and lesser lights for the darkness? Wouldn't you think that I would make as great a light for the darkness as I did for the day? Yes, the daylight is for work, and the night lights are for rest—but there is more.

The lesser lights bring a message in the darkness—a warning and a help—to brighten the dark and lead you through it.

Often in life, you go through periods of darkness—maybe you experience fear or confusion, times where you question and seek direction. But then, because of the smaller, lesser lights, you can find your way. They are symbolic of My hand and My voice leading you and helping you along the way.

As you pull your covers up over you at night—especially if you are experiencing fear—you can find safety and comfort in the lesser lights of circumstance, those visits I give you in your darkness. Don't wait in fear for the bright light of day. Recognize My help and comfort in the little things—a friend who offers wisdom, a heart that shares your feelings and offers understanding, a loving hug that gives comfort, or wise counsel from another. All of these small, unexpected, and often unrecognized touches are from the lesser lights in your darkness.

So seek and find My love, Presence, and understanding in every trial. I never leave you alone but offer help in many different ways. If your heart or your spirit is not open to seeing that, the darkness will just seem darker. So look for the lesser lights—look for My hand, My love, and My comfort. That is why I lead you to move and offer help and comfort to others. In this way, you actually become the lesser light.

You'll never be alone, and I will always be with you. Recognize Me in the little lights I bring to you and offer thanks because it is I Who bring the light."

THE SUN NEVER MOVES

"THE SUN IS setting. It looks like it is sinking below the horizon. Angels surround it, glorifying Me. But it is the earth that is really moving. The sun never moves. Neither do I.

I am the Son of God. So if the light is not as bright for you, who moved? You wonder where I went without realizing that I am always the same, 'Yesterday, today, and forever.' (Hebrews 13:8 KJB) And I always desire your presence.

Your concept of Me is determined by wordly influences. These either condemn you or accept you depending upon your mood and your circumstances.

Your faith is robbed and you sink into depression.

Are you worried? Unhappy? Scared? Check your thoughts, they are feeding your emotions. This is why praising Me is always the answer. It is not just for Me but for you—because it is the way to happiness in your mind. It exists to keep you filled with truth and joy.

Many wonder why praise is so important. It is because I love you, and I want you to be happy and trust Me. Praise is the best, most absolute way to have a free and happy mind. It expresses trust in Me and My unlimited love for you.

Come to Me, draw closer and closer, you'll find that your praise and trust will change your experience by giving you a new and brighter look on the horizon. Be at peace and keep your eyes on the Son."

THE WHISPERING EAR

THIS MORNING I read the scripture, "I will counsel you with My eye upon you." (Psalm 32:8 ESV) Then, I saw the Lord whispering in an ear.

"I speak in a still small voice. It is odd that silence can carry and draw more attention than noise. Listen for Me. I am there, speaking. Listen, do you see the intense closeness of the whisper? The familiarity, the care, the counsel? I share your life with you and I am eager for this relationship. I give you counsel, but do you hear? When I speak, it will draw you closer and deeper to Me. If it causes unrest, condemnation, or contrary feelings, it is not Me. So guard your ears. You will hear Me if you are willing. Turning your ear to Me involves turning your heart. Be willing. Listen. My voice will not come from the outside but from the heart. It will heal, love, restore, guide, forgive, and correct, but never condemn.

My heart dwells in your heart. If you close your eyes, listen for its beat, you will find it in the peace and love you feel. Believe. I am not what man has created Me to be. I am peace, love, joy, patience, kindness, gentleness, faithfulness, goodness, self control, and forgiveness. If you are not feeling these, it is not Me. Listen. You will find Me calling you, ready and willing to hold you, forgive you, and counsel you, for 'My eye is always upon you.' (Psalm 102:19 ESV) Just listen."

FRUITFULNESS

"YES, HEAVEN IS coming to destroy evil. But on the horizon, there are also flames of fire. For where the evil is destroyed, I will replenish the earth. I will cleanse it by My fire to bring revival and the fire of My love. The revival will, by its very nature, cleanse the earth of the remnants of evil. The damage will be replenished with new things, things never seen or heard. A life fuller than that which has ever been known will arrive. Yet even in its glory, it will only be as a teaspoon on the earth compared to the coming of My Kingdom.

Imagine a life filled with fruitfulness, real fruit, always ripe, ready to eat. This is My desire. To see goodness manifested in My children—love for one another, the purpose in each day being to serve, provide, and bless all who surround you. To heal, to minister to every need by My Spirit with confident faith in Me to minister with you. Where faith is without question. Where doubt doesn't exist. Where My glory is always revealed as you pray.

Imagine a heart that is always filled and ready. A mind with an understanding that moves faith into realms it has never known. The birth of My Kingdom is still within you—in the womb. Nourish it by My Word and soak in Me. And the day will come when all that is unseen will be seen."

PRAISE BECOMES WORSHIP

"'GREAT IS THE Lord and greatly to be praised.' (Psalm 48:1ESV) Praise is the key ingredient. Praise does not only come in shouts, cymbals, instruments, and dance, it comes from a deep, personal knowledge of Me.

Just as you've learned to recognize My voice in that deep place within you, you will also notice deep praise coming out of that place in a silent, unspeakable voice.

There is praise in the soul that is expressed in the body, and there is praise that brings your face to the floor.

That core in you, that place that no one else can reach reaches into eternity and joins heavenly choirs. It is a place that earth can never know.

But you know. That place of communion. The joining of heaven and earth. It is where the Holy Spirit dwells.

My deepest desire is to share in the lives of My children. Draw near, be still, surrender your world, and listen. You will meet Me here, and praise will overflow from your heavenly core and bless your life."

GO AHEAD—SURRENDER

IN MY PRAYER time this morning, I was drawn to think about how Jesus so willingly relinquished His life and submitted to death. He submitted to the proud, the arrogant, the jeering, the mockery, the whipping, and the nails. And then, He died. I can't get past that. The God Who created us gave Himself over to evil men for His own suffering and destruction, giving up all of His rightful glory and honor to lay it all down…and die…for all for us.

I've heard this my whole life, but I guess I concentrated more on the Cross, the Blood, Salvation and the Resurrection. I never really contemplated His surrender to death. The surrender of the God of the universe, in Jesus, Who is all truth, to death, takes my breath away.

I think I always just concentrated on, "He paid the price for us," (Galatians 3:13 GW) "By His stripes we were healed," (1 Peter 2:24 KJV) "He cleansed us from all sin," (1 John 1:7 NLT) "We have passed from judgment to life." (John 5:24 NKJV) But…God dying?! You are probably thinking I'm really slow. I mean 49 years to realize this? I guess I just went from the Cross to the Resurrection. I just never stayed in the tomb.

I mean, God dying and becoming so "helpless"…talk about laying it all down! What kind of love is that? How could I ever doubt? I think it's not just that He died, it's that He willfully laid His life down to death, a place of no control, no retaliation, no fight, no compromise…He just surrendered all.

Surrender? I think we may all have things in our daily life that, even unwittingly, are not surrendered—where our flesh rises up, our will is challenged, our hearts struggle. I know I do.

That word, surrender, has a new meaning for me now. Lord, help me surrender all to You.

THE INNER EAR

"THERE ARE TWO ways to hear. One, with the outer, external ear that can hear and record it in your brain, and the other, with the inner ear of the heart that becomes a womb that will bring forth life.

Don't just memorize the Word, let it sink deep into your being where it can do its work. Simmer each part of the Word and its meaning till it becomes like a fine meal that you will never forget. Don't rush, 'eat' slowly, and it will fill and refresh your whole being. It isn't the number of verses that you learn but the meaning of those verses that brings you life.

You have heard, 'You become what you eat.' Apply that to your heart, and you will become what you were created to be—fulfill your destiny."

YOUR BARKING DOG

"WHO IS IT that makes you miserable? Who is it that robs you of faith, joy, and confidence? Who is it that interferes with My work in you like a dog barking and rumbling at your feet? You know who it is—it's the devil—so why do you pay attention to him? He is a liar and a thief. He has no interest in you but to steal all I have given you. Stop him, face him with the truth you know. The truth I have given you. Let all his lies go, or they will rot your soul. You are stronger than that. Stand straight. He thinks he is Goliath, but you can destroy his work with the rock of your foundation. THE NAME of JESUS! Use it, and My name will do its work. Praise, sing, and trust My truth. TRUST! Think about that."

FRUITFUL EVANGELISM

WATCHING GOOD THINGS happen to others or watching others who are doing good things always brings tears and a smile. Goodness just naturally seems to bring peace and happiness.

It makes me wonder: how do we truly evangelize people in talking about Jesus?

Do we say, "You're a sinner. You're going to hell. You better receive Jesus or else?"

Even though the bottom line is true, it's not the whole story. God does hate sin, and there isn't one of us who hasn't sinned in one way or another, sin is sin. But the only reason He hates sin is because He loves us so much!!! Sin separates us from Him so **He went after it with His life!!**

He left His throne and went to the cross with inhuman torture along the way. He paid the price and penalty of sin Himself to destroy that separation.

He came to save, not condemn.

"For by grace you have been saved, through fath—and this is not from yourselves, it is the gift of God, not the result of works so that no one can boast." (Ephesians 2:8-9 NIV)

We are not saved by works but by turning from our sin, believing in Him in faith, accepting His death in our place, and receiving Jesus and His finished work of love in our heart. That's what brings us to Him and our heavenly home.

I cry God's tears for those who need the wonderful mercy God offers. From the most well-thought-of person in the world to the most beaten down, addicted, mentally ill, deprived, merciless person on earth, His mercy is the cry of His heart, His ache, His pain is to save us, and it will always be there for those who turn to Him.

DEEPER REVELATION

"DO YOU WANT a deeper revelation of who I am? Do you want to increase your awareness of My presence? Then seek it. Spend time with Me. A relationship doesn't come automatically. Does your evening meal just appear on the table, or do you have to make it? It takes effort, planning, work.

This is to be a relationship, a marriage. Marriage is made of love. We need to have time alone, time to share and express our love. I don't just want your faith isolated in a belief system. And I don't just want your time for its own sake. I want to share My love with you, and in that, let you know how deep that love goes. In the beginning, I move you along like a baby in a carriage, but as you learn to walk with Me, walking in rhythm, our relationship will grow. Don't run ahead or fall behind, move with Me. As you yield your life to Me, you will find the path I have prepared for you. I never work against you I work with you and for you. I created you from My heart, and My heart yearns for you to give Me yours. In this, you will find the revelation you seek.

I will never leave you, I will only draw you on—deeper into Me and for eternity."

I AM YOUR FATHER

"WHEN I SAY I am your Father, do you really know what I mean? I held you in My heart long before you were born. I focused on every part of you. I know your heart, your mind, your hopes, dreams, weaknesses, and ways. I formed it all. I gave you a dream, a vision, and all you need to accomplish it. I did not make you to be frustrated but fulfilled. I made you to fit the plan I had for you.

But then—sin came.

As a result, My creation in, around, and for you, became infected. Your heart knows its purpose, yet it is bound and misdirected both by the sin of the world and the distorted vision you have of yourself.

But then—the Cross and Resurrection!

The vision and possibilities are restored. My glory is waiting to be revealed in you—waiting to see My vision for you revealed.

Only believe.

My original creation in you is like weary old bones that crack when you start to move. They've been bound for so long. But now, you can move by faith into who you really are. Don't be afraid, I will help you stand and function according to My original plan.

Your dreams? From me.

Your unused abilities? Use them.

Your hopes? They are My vision.

Wake up. Stand up. Do it—one step at a time. Just do what comes naturally, and find time to enjoy who you really are."

THE MISSING BRICKS

IN MY PRAYER time, I saw a brick wall with missing bricks here and there. And the Lord said…

"The bricks are your strength. The missing spaces are your weaknesses. Those weaknesses are all and each because of your lack of understanding of Who I am.

Yes, I created the world. But that's where most people stop. Think about that world. I hold in My Hands the depths of the earth. Observe and take in My world—its beauty, its power, and how everything is fed in, through, and by My creation, even the air you breathe.

'The heavens proclaim My glory.' (Psalm 19:1NLT) 'Shout to the Lord all the earth. Break out and praise, and sing for joy. Let the sea and everything in it shout His praise. Let the earth and all living things join in. Let the rivers clap their hands in glee. Let the hills sing for joy before the Lord.' (Psalm 98:4, 7-8 NLT)

Is there any other god who can say this? No. 'You are My witnesses, My servants whom I have chosen, in order that you may know Me, believe in Me, and understand that I am He. Before Me there was no other God formed, and there will be none after Me.' (Isaiah 43:10 NIV)

Fill those empty places with new bricks of understanding of Who I am and the mystery of My power. Then the next time you pray, let your faith reach in and rest in that understanding.

I hold the whole earth and all it contains. I rule all of its movements, power, comfort, and sustenance. How then, can you ever doubt that I will hear your prayers?

I have already sent the answer. His name is Jesus. Only believe."

I KNOW YOU

"I AM YOUR Father—I know you, I love you, and I do what is best for you. I do not just give orders or commandments and let our relationship depend on your obedience. When you hear My voice, you obey, and that pleases Me—but it does not end there.

No, keeping the Commandments is your expression of love for Me. This is the Father/child relationship.

Do you struggle with angry thoughts, hurts, or unforgiveness? Come, talk with Me, and I will listen to you and help you through it, because I understand you.

Don't try to make yourself perfect before you come to Me. Come to Me, and I will show you the Way to perfection.

When I ask you to understand each other, do you not think I want you to know I understand you? Moving deeper into My love means moving into deeper communion with Me. You cannot know My love if you don't know Me. I look and listen for you. Turn to Me with all your heart and with all that's in your heart, and you will find that My understanding brings healing, forgiveness, and a deeper understanding of My love for you."

THE MELODY OF LIFE

"MELODY. DO YOU ever marvel at the miracle of it? It isn't just a sound but the life and ministry it carries. Who can imagine where that melody comes from? There is a sound in heaven that can permeate the earth, and it comes naturally. The air is filled with it, it can make its way into hearts that are ready to receive it.

If you want to experience My life released in you, you have only to let your heart move to the 'sound' it hears. Just as a melody is heard in the heart of the musician, so the melody of your life is heard within you—your dreams, visions, or desires to do something, write something, or give something from within yourself.

Are you frustrated in your life? Do you feel unfulfilled? Maybe your energy is used up by worldly needs. Find time—it's there, I promise you— carry our relationship with you, and you will have all day to be with Me. Let Me reveal the core of that frustration. I want you to know the joy of being you.

I have put that vision and the ability in you. Don't let it stay buried— make room for it. Use it. Do it. Enjoy it."

PONDER MY GREATNESS

"WHEN YOU COME to Me and receive the saving grace of My cross, the healing of My stripes, and the assurance of salvation, you might think that's all there is to know. But I want you to know more—there are depths in My creation that you will never understand. It is all too vast for you. But the lack of revelation is, in itself, a revelation of depths you will never know or even see of My creation.

I want you to ponder My greatness—to know the kind of power that works toward you—to give you life, feed you, give you air to breathe, beauty and designs that are never-ending, life in seas that are too deep to even imagine, and eternity that reaches into places unimagined. I want you to know that this God—this God Who made all things—things you can't even begin to understand, loves you. It is that simple. My greatness, My power at work in you, toward you, and for you.

How feeble that makes your smallest hope sound. I've told you, you can use this power to move mountains. So rise up! Get bold in your prayers. Turn your hope to powerful, expectant faith—speak out great things. Don't settle for your smallest need—speak and expect powerful, life-changing things. Use it to bless others—to bring My greatness into tired, young, and old hurting lives.

Next time your faith seems frail, just look at My creation and ponder My greatness. It is there for you—to encourage and empower you to pray great prayers!"

THE POWER WITHIN YOU

"YOU ARE IN Me. I am in you. Have you really contemplated that? I, the only living, powerful, creator God, live in you. How then, can you doubt My power? Or, My Promises? If we are one, why do you think your prayers are 'your' prayers? What you face, we face together. I lead and initiate your prayers and bring you through the confusion of fear and need—to the prayer that will deliver you.

No need for signs—just experience My presence in each day with you. We are one…so guard against that thief who would try to divide us by tempting you with unbelief.

When you look at creation, you are filled with the reality of My power and creativity. So then, turn your face to Me—look beyond your mind into your spirit, and let My power and creativity inspire your thoughts, visions, and solutions. Pay attention to the inspiration you get, the desire to pray, the burden to do or say something that will bring blessings…these things come from Who I am in you. I use the gift you are to bring about all that I am."

A POWERFUL NEW RIVER

I SAW A river that turned from its course and started flowing into a desert.

"No one is ready for what is coming. Get ready—make ready by preparing your heart to be open. Fertilize it with My word and listen in prayer.

For a surge of My Spirit is coming to cleanse and empower My body. It will open cisterns that lie closed at the bottom of your heart. Prepare for My river to reach those places that have been shut by unbelief, discouragement, and yes, laziness. Pray for hunger to strengthen you to open the door—then I will fill it as never before. This is not a refreshment but an outpouring you have never known or seen.

Put aside doubt, unbelief, mental understanding, and lay your heart open before Me. If you limit Me by your understanding, you limit this river to the limitations of your mind. Prepare, be ready—it is coming—it has made its turn and is beginning to flow. Prepare to embrace the Holy Spirit and immerse yourself in His power."

SPINNING YOUR WHEELS

"YOU'VE HEARD THE saying, 'You are just spinning your wheels and getting nowhere.' But have you tried putting your wheels on the ground?

When you confess faith without really expecting, it is just like spinning your wheels. So how do you put those wheels on the ground? First of all, you have to realize that the ground is My Word; so put them on My Word and My truth with confidence. If you pedal a stationary bike are you going anywhere? If you pedal a bike with its wheels on the ground, what a difference it makes. One gets you nowhere, and one gets you anywhere you want to go. Any direction, whether it's level, low, or high ground. This is a picture of faith. How do you put your faith on the ground? You move forward toward what you believe. It starts with your heart—absorb its truth—then it is moved by your supporting thoughts. Your thoughts lead to hope and hope to expectation—each is a turn of the wheel, which with practice, will move more quickly and easily until you obtain a consistent speed.

You really 'pedal' faith. You push it, you know it will cause motion, you don't let your mind put the brakes on by negative activity.

Picture a tandem bike with both of us together. I'm right behind you, supporting you, and moving in your faith. If I'm in front, you are not going in faith, I am. But I train you to be strong—so you know how to move in faith—all the while knowing that you are never alone and I am always with you. So push hard, pedal that faith I have given you. Don't listen to the negative mind—follow your faith-filled heart."

NOTHING IS APART FROM ME

"I COME ON a cloud. I fill the earth. All will see Me. All will know the truth that I am. I don't just speak the truth—I am the truth. I am in all things. There is nothing apart from Me that did not exist before—in Me.

As a woman gives birth to a baby who has been fed and nurtured by her very being, so all of My creation has been nurtured in Me. That is why you can feel such a relationship with creation—it is a manifested part of Me; I am present in it. And it witnesses to the world that I AM. It groans to see My glory because it longs for the world to know Me and My great love for you.

There is nothing that is apart from Me. As you go through your day, check your steps to see what I have provided for you. You will not find one thing that did not originate in Me. My creation constantly caresses you with the gifts it offers. The more you become aware of those gifts, the more you will find Me in the blessings of My creation.

Go outside, take a deep breath, and breathe Me in. The more you do this, the more you will treasure My presence in every moment and in everything you see. You will not need to see Me coming on a cloud to cry, 'Glory.' I am before you every day. The purpose of prayer is not just for the sake of satisfying needs. It is a sharing in the desires of My heart, giving voice and agreement with the good I desire to bring.

Do you think these are your desires? No. It is My will at work in you. And the good you seek for others is the good I want for you as well.

My greatest desire is that you would truly know and understand My love. Fear and awe of Me is because of My glory and the power contained in Me. But love for Me comes from knowing that My greatest power is in My love for you."

SUBMIT YOUR SPIRIT TO ME

"I HAVE LISTENED to your prayers and seen your struggle to put words on what your heart feels. As a result, you feel like you are just rambling, and at times, you are. But more importantly, I have heard your heart. I know its intensity and its earnest desires.

Can you remember times when you just sat before Me and couldn't express your feelings? Maybe you just cried and had no words to explain your thoughts. That is the best place to be when you pray. Give Me your heart and the words will come. You must submit your soul (mind) to your spirit—then expression will follow, and it will bring peace and clarity.

The things in your soul can become confused, distorted, and in that, lose meaning. But if you surrender that confusion to the spirit, it will become clear, simple, and illuminated. The spirit must always rule. The soul has led for a long time and rebels against giving up leadership. But now, your spirit has been resurrected and has taken over bringing My peace. All confusion comes from the soul, but if you surrender it to Me, in your spirit, you will gain great light, your prayers will have greater power, and you will understand what your soul cannot grasp.

Do you think I will ever refuse an earnest prayer? My whole being has longed from the beginning of time to hear you. You were created for this— that you would come to Me and call Me Father. You are the love of My life. You are the reason for creation. It is all for you—and has been formed to surround you with My love and provision. Do you not think I treasure your earnest prayers? Prayers that seek more of Me and have a passion to know Me better? Prayers that seek good for others? Understand that when you intercede that way, it is I Who am moving in you and through you for them."

PREPARE YOURSELF

"ABRAHAM STAGGERED NOT at the promises of God but gave glory to God and was strengthened in his faith." (Romans 4:20 KJV 1900)

"Do you stagger at My promises? Does your faith reach to that which you cannot begin to understand? Or, is your faith limited by the confusion of your soul?

I call you to faith. Today. Look up and see that which seems impossible; reach up and plant your faith in a higher place. When I walked the earth, deaf ears were opened, the blind could see, legs that couldn't move began to walk.

I have left you markers of truth. Do you want to know what you're to do? Just follow My markers, and do what I did and more.

The time for preparation is now:

> Purify your hearts daily
> Follow your heart
> Listen to your peace
> Obey
> Trust

"'For I the Lord thy God will hold thy right hand, saying unto thee, 'Fear not, I will help thee.'" (Isaiah 41:13 ERV)"

COME UNDER MY WATERFALL

"MY WORD IS always going forth. The Bible is like a waterfall, always flowing, but not all come near, see, or receive its blessing.

My Word to you has been poured out—ready to heal, cleanse, and save. But more than that, it has been poured out to bring us into relationship together, alone in intimate understanding.

As a waterfall fills the rivers, it provides a place of both rest and wonder. Some will immerse themselves in this river, and others will just rest on top. It is all up to you. My call goes out to all, for I am so ready and eager to share My heart with all of My children.

You will see that the more you seek to understand Me, the more treasure you will find. The more treasure you find, the more My heart is filled with joy. If you only knew how precious it is for Me to have time with you.

'In Me you can live and move and have your being.' (Acts 17:28 NIV) I love this—how wonderful to live in an ongoing intimate relationship filled with joy, laughter, teaching, and revelation, just passing between us moment by moment.

Come under My waterfall, be filled with My Word. Get to know Me in this intimate way. Be filled with both the knowledge and the experience of My great love for you together with My blessing and personal care.

Just keep coming to Me—come and be refreshed and make My joy complete."

BLESSING THE LORD

"BLESS THE LORD O my soul, and let all that is within me bless His Holy Name." (Psalm 103:1 ESV)

Our blessing Him has nothing to do with our needs or our prayers. We bless Him simply because of Who He is. We bless Him because He is God, Creator of the universe, King of all kings, Lord of heaven and earth, and He is worthy of praise.

His mighty power and glory bring us to our knees no matter what is going on in our lives. He is worthy of praise, and we fall down before Him just because of Who He is.

"Who is this King of Glory? The Lord of heaven's armies—He is the King of Glory." (Psalm 24:10 NLT)

"You are worthy oh Lord to receive glory and honor and power, for You created all things and by Your will they exist and were created." (Revelation 4:11 NLT)

"The heavens proclaim the glory of God. The skies display His craftsmanship. Day after day they continue to speak; night after night they make Him known. They speak without a sound or word; their voice is never heard. Yet their message has gone throughout the earth, and their words to all the world." (Psalm 19:1-4 NLT)

And what does the King of glory say to us?

"When you call out to Me I will answer you. I will be with you in trouble. I will rescue you and give you honor." (Psalm 91:15 NLT)

"So in my distress I cried out to the Lord, yes, I prayed to my God for help. He heard me from His sanctuary; my cry to Him reached His ears." (Psalm 18: NLT)

"The Lord thundered from heaven; the voice of the Most High resounded amid the hail and burning coals. Then at Your command, oh Lord, at the blast of Your breath, the bottom of the sea could be seen and the foundations of the earth were laid bare. He reached down from heaven and rescued me. He drew me out of deep waters. He rescued me from my powerful enemy, and He took me to a place of safety." (Psalm 18:13-19 NLT)

THE WOBBLY WHEEL

"SEE A TRAIN with many wheels? One wheel isn't working—it is just kind of flopping like a flat tire even though it is made of iron. It is causing a whole railroad car to wobble and not move as fast as it can.

There is tremendous power in the train, but it can't operate at its full potential—all because of just one wheel not working at its capacity.

Do you not realize how important you are? Do you not realize that, 'Now it is God who makes both us and you stand firm in Christ. He anointed us, set His seal of ownership on us, and put His Spirit in our hearts as a deposit, guaranteeing what is to come.' (2 Corinthians 1:21-22 NIV)

There is no one who is more or less important than you are. You have to encourage each other to pick up your individual gifts and use them. Each must function at its best or My glory will not be seen.

Don't let the devil and his same old lies deter you from moving in the full power of My Spirit. You know he is a thief, so don't pay attention to the lie he is using to rob you. TRUST in ME to fulfill your call. You prove your trust by your obedience.

So Obey My work in your heart. Don't be afraid. Move with Me. Don't hold back My work in you. Fear only comes from depending on yourself. Depend on Me and you will come to new heights."

BARRENNESS

"BARREN. BARREN WILDERNESS. Barren womb. Barren heart. Barren vision. Barren life. Barren—empty, without life.

Almost everyone is barren somewhere. Aa place that is void of love, productivity, hope, dreams, fulfillment. There is just an emptiness, an undefined or understood emptiness. Either way, there is a place in you that yearns for more.

This barrenness comes from a lack somewhere. Neglect, hurt, circumstances that rob you and leave you empty. It can be just from receiving nothing. No seeds have been planted. A lack of approval, appreciation or encouragement leaves an emptiness that aches to grow into something—but empty soil only brings weeds.

Give Me your emptiness. I will fill it. I leave nothing undone or untouched. Give Me that hope, that yearning, that hurt or need, that dream. Then watch the fruit grow as I plant My seeds of love and hope and vision. Watch as I bring to life that which has been dormant from neglect or pain. Be healed. Be filled. Be who I say you are, not others. Don't look back. Look forward and see a new vision.

'May you experience the love of Christ, though it is too great to understand fully.

Then you will be made complete with all the fullness of life and power that comes from God.' (Ephesians 3:19 NLT)"

THE ATTACK ON PEACE

"PEACE. WHEN YOU have true peace your joy is full. But scattered thoughts, worries, plans, memories—all of these are like scattered seeds that are tossed throughout your being. Good things, bad things, all running around inside you, having their way while interrupting your inner peace. The devil likes to toss these thoughts and reminders around like confetti, leaving you to deal with them. He gets your spirit, soul, and body to work in conflict with each other. The result is confusion and frustration. See them like waves on the sea. Use your authority saying, 'Peace, be still.' (Mark 4:39 KJB) Put them to rest and trust Me to bring order.

Keep your spirit (heart) set on Me to bring order to your day. Bring your soul (mind) into submission to your spirit, and the body will follow and be free to rest.

Whether you have much to do or little to do, it is the heart that must reign. Focus your thoughts on My Word. Allow yourself to settle in My love, and peace will walk through the day with you. Keep your heart—not your mind—open to My leading, and your day will be filled with the joy of walking and doing your work with Me. Look for the things that bring life. Life will always lead and encourage you."

HOW TO WEAR HIS ARMOR

"DON'T MAKE MY armor a physical act or activity. Just…
>Give yourself to Me
>Speak the truth
>Know My Word
>Act righteously
>Trust and believe
>Be at peace by walking with Me.

>Receive My saving grace every day.

Wearing this armor (Ephesians 6:11NKJV) will in effect, be preaching the gospel. And preaching it in love. For it is My love that brings the gospel.

Do this to the world and to each other. Let your armor be a shining light that opens hearts to Me.

Nothing resists evil more than doing good. By doing this, it will bring protection to you by deflating the enemy and exposing his tactics. Just act in love."

FILLING GOD WITH JOY

"ARE YOU FULL? I am filled with joy from your praise. I know your heart, I hear you, and I see you. And so, I shall return this fullness to you and let its blessings be upon you.

I gave you My life, therefore, you have life. I do not keep and absorb your praise to Myself—it will always return with My blessings.

You will not falter, you will move ahead to new places—to places I have prepared and designed for you. Do you think your praise affects only Me? No, your praises are steps on a stairway to Me.

Know that your faith has called you forward. It not only moves in your prayer, but it brings you to a higher place. You are never alone, I am always with you, so you need not fear. I will help you understand the deeper ways and show you places you have never been. Then, I will bring you even higher. For I dwell in your praises, so where I am, you will also be."

CHANGING GOD'S DESIGN

"SEE THE TREE? The man is cutting its branches. It is not to prune it or perfect its growth—it is to redesign it to fit the man's purpose.

Its beauty is lost, its own joy is gone. Yet it continues in its attempt to thrive and be what it can be.

I see this happen with My children. Parents, friends, teachers—and all with good intentions—try to form My children to their own pattern. 'You should do this or you should do that.' 'Bend this way, bend that way.' Imagine being encouraged and allowed to just do what comes naturally—to grow and blossom according to the pattern I have put in them. Guide means to help along, not re-form.

Look at those people in your life, whether children or adults, and guide them by encouraging what you see developing as they move through their lives, producing beauty, fruit, or excellence. Let them be who they are—help them grow and find joy in who I created them to be. For they are formed for a purpose, and it shall be used for all eternity. Don't reshape My world—help its natural beauty to be revealed."

SEE IT AS FINISHED

"I HAVE MADE all things clean. When I saved and restored you, I saved and restored the world I created. It is Mine. I have cleansed it. You are Mine. I have cleansed you. Live and walk with the knowledge that you are clean. The work of the cross has been finished. See it that way.

Just as you are waiting to see the finished work so too, creation waits, but the work has been done. Yes, you have to walk and work out your salvation, but I see it as finished. So should you. This is where your joy will come from. I have done the work. You have received it. Your only work is to believe in Me.

Take that faith and make it as a shield. Most see that shield as protection from attacks. But you must also see it as protection from yourself, your mind and your actions. Living in faith does not just mean miracles—it means trusting and loving in all circumstances, it means submitting to My heart and being obedient to the promptings of the Holy Spirit. Do all the good things your faith prompts you to do."

IS TRUST AN EXPERIENCE?

"TRUST. WHAT DOES it mean to you? Think on that one word today—trust. How and where does it fit into your life? Is it just a word you use to encourage your mind? Or is it an actual experience in your heart? Find its definition within you. Is it something you are trying to do, or is it something that simply resides in and rules your spirit?

Find one need or worry today—and start applying trust to those thoughts or that situation. How do you feel? If there is no peace, there is no trust.

If you begin to praise Me for that 'need,' you will find that peace will seep in, and trust will begin to manifest itself within you.

Praise is always the key ingredient in every prayer. It's true—Trust Me."

LIGHTS. LANTERNS. LIGHTNING

"THE NECESSITY OF light. When light comes, it illuminates the darkness, but different variations and brightnesses determine how much you see. The sun is too bright to look at directly, but too little light will cloud the understanding. The eyesight also will determine how much and how clearly you see.

It can be the same with the spirit. This is why you may only learn a little at a time. But as light increases, so does the understanding. And when the understanding increases, so does the power. The eye is then able to look at even brighter light—this is revelation. However, revelation would not have come without the foundation of the lesser lights.

Every time you read My Word, spend time in prayer, or ponder creation, your light will increase. Clouds will move and understanding with knowledge will come. It may start as a flash of lightning or as the sun beaming through a cloud. But it will all bring you to Me, the light of the world.

I have given you so many ways to see. Don't settle for the dim thoughts or ideas as if that's all there are, but take the lesser light, draw closer, seek to see, write it down, bring it all together. In this writing, you will be amazed to find how I can speak to you and bring more revelation as you write your thoughts on a scripture, an observation, or a thought process.

Seek My voice in all things, for I love to speak with you. This relationship is why I came, and I treasure every time you turn to Me with a listening ear. As we grow in this relationship, the light within you will grow brighter and brighter and as your heart grows more and more open, you will see the day when you will be able to look at the sun."

HOW TO LIVE IN PEACE

"PEACE. BE AT peace. Let it come. Let it rule. All other emotions fight to rule. Make them submit to you and allow peace to reign.

I have given you My peace—it is not an object or even a belief. It is Myself—My Presence that pulsates within you, bringing the activity and noise within you to rest. If you focus on My Presence, you will find that peace comes naturally, without thought. This is the place of trust—knowing that I love you, that I rule your life with My goodness, and that I will lead you through all the 'mines' of worry and fear the devil would try to put on you.

Destroy the mines with My Word. When these lies assail you, use My Word to resist them, and you will see them dissolve under its power.

For I AM the Word. Envision that. So when you speak it, you are declaring My Presence in what you speak. And with My Presence comes My authority. Draw a picture of this in your mind. **When you speak My Word, you are announcing My Presence in you and the truth of Who I am and what I have declared as truth for you. The devil will flee, and you will find peace.**"

A DAM

"A DAM. WATER is pouring through a large central hole. The water has the power to enlarge the hole and eventually break down the whole dam. What is stopping it?

There are things that have been in you for years preventing the pressure of the water of My Spirit to have its way. This prevention is not because the wall is stronger than the water but because your own will won't allow it. You pray for more of Me and more of My Holy Spirit yet you prohibit anything you don't understand. You have a filter that works in you that you don't even know is there. It just naturally resists any increase of the Spirit that you can't explain.

I want more for you. And you want more, too. But you have a natural resistance to anything new. You confuse discernment with your own judgment. Can't you trust Me? 'Would I give you a stone instead of bread?' (Matthew 7:9 ESV) Do you think you already have all that I want to give you?

Give Me free reign in your life—you will experience and begin to function far beyond what you can imagine. Let your wall come down. Allow My Spirit to become a constant 'waterfall' in your life and in your prayers.

Miracles will no longer be a distant hope—allow My presence to move and increase your power.

My love will never leave you. But My love also desires for you to grow in your knowledge of Me so that I can use you in increasing measure."

DON'T LIMIT LOVE

"DO YOU THINK I do not see the anguish of your soul or the pain you hold in your heart? Do you think I judge every thought—every weight of pressure? Don't allow the limitations of your love to limit your understanding of Mine.

For the depths of the ocean are shallow compared to My love. There is no end to My understanding. I want to share your life, not be your dictator. To wash you with kindness, not a whip of judgment. To share and heal your heart, to relieve your inner pressure, to wash away your self-deprecation, to lift you up and cleanse the worldly dust. Have faith in Me, not in a doctrine or a 'way' designed by man. Have faith in Me. Meditate on My love at Calvary—enter into it and see that there is no bottom to its depth—it has no limits."

MY WORLD

"WHEN YOU CAME into My world, what did you see? A world you didn't understand—it meant nothing to you. The only thing you wanted was to have every need satisfied. Then you looked around and began to wonder, and that wonder will never stop. So much to learn, to understand. But then, there's that one thing you will never need to understand—it becomes an experience—and that is love. It can affect your whole life's course. It can change your mind, your future, and your whole being. It is unseen and intangible. But it holds the greatest power in the world.

You can experience My love everywhere. That is, if you look for it. It might come gradually as you slowly observe all the things I have made, or it may come quickly, unexpectedly, when you become enraptured, just for a moment, in the indescribable beauty of a petal on a flower. Its simplicity defies explanation. Men might discover the how but never the why. Why this petal? Why all the others like it? Why so many different kinds and colors? What do they do? Or say? Who can understand the heart of its designer—The Creator?

Look around, find My heart, and you will begin to see it everywhere. Man wants to explain everything. I want you to experience everything. As you do, you'll find more and more mysteries, you will be more and more amazed, and you will be surrounded by My glory. The experience of love in My Creation will go deeper and deeper as you soak in My presence and in all that I have made."

A LARGE ARM CHAIR

I SAW A large arm chair…It was the judgment seat of Christ. Then I heard…

"What do you think about judgment? I want you to understand what it really is. It is the separation of the wheat and the tares, the sorting out of believers from unbelievers, the washed from the unclean.

Do you know the pain of this judgment for Me? How hard it is for Me to see this? For it is not really I who judge you, but you who judge yourselves. You do this by rejecting Me and the gift of My life for you. It is not My will that any be judged and separated from Me. But the choice has been made—and it was made by you. People fear judgment, yet again, the choice is not Mine but yours. You can choose life—choose to live forever with Me. I already made the choice to save you, to die for your sins and take the penalty on Myself. Now all you have to do is choose Me. Receive the gift of life. To reject Me is to reject that gift. And when you do, My heart breaks. Imagine your child rejecting you. And I am even more to you. For I am your Creator; I formed you, I called you by name, with the full intention of spending eternity with you.

So don't fear judgment, fear yourself. For you are really judging yourself by rejecting My gift, My life—My Fatherhood. I love you and call you to come to Me ready to enter eternal life in the place I have prepared for you—to be filled with and surrounded by My never-ending love.

'Very truly I tell you, whoever hears My word and believes Him who sent Me has eternal life and will not be charged but has crossed over from death to life.'" (John 5:24 NIV)

WELLSPRING

"THERE IS A well. It is only as deep as you are willing to dig and its depths are yours for the taking. You can drink as much as you want, it has no bottom, and it will never run dry. However, it might never be used.

How deep are you willing to dig? How hungry are you to drink of its blessings? Are you willing to make room in your heart by eliminating those things that crowd it or pollute it? You are in charge of its purity.

I have prepared this water for you. My goodness has gone ahead and filled the ground on which you walk because this well will go with you wherever you go. Close your eyes and think, for it is within you. It is in My Presence, in My Holy Spirit that resides in you. How wonderful when we can drink together. I offer it to you daily, even when you think the well is dry and its fullness evades you. This happens because your mind has taken control and clouds your hungry heart. Learn to let the purity of The Holy Spirit rule, for His well is always ready to quench your thirst. When the mind wants to be satisfied, it robs you of the truth that you know deep inside of you. Remember, the devil can use your mind but not your spirit—not when it belongs to Me. Which one do you want to hear?"

ALL ARE SWINGING

"SWINGS—WIDE ONES. EVERYONE'S swinging at different speeds and heights. But all are swinging. No one is idle. This is My body. All are growing and moving at different speeds and times. But while the swings are wide enough for two, even three people, some only have one person sitting in them. Why is that?

There are others, those who sit on a bench, alone, with a stranger, or just watching, thinking, wishing, or hurting. Reach out to them, invite them to join you. You all have a testimony. You all have knowledge of Me, so share it. And do that with My love, not your expertise or fancy deep words, just My love. Do I love you? How do you know? Just share that. Swing at your own speed and height but swing.

Touch people with kindness. That is the door that will always open a heart. Don't jump into words, just be kind and thoughtful. In time, your testimony will be welcomed not admonished. Be real. Learn to evangelize from the heart, not memorized verses.

True evangelism is simply sharing My love, for it is love that brought the testimony. That experience of My love is, in a sense, the Word made flesh that was manifested in Jesus. If they first find Me in you, they will listen to My Word."

PRAISE BRINGS LIFE

"CAN YOU IMAGINE this world—even the universe—if it was filled with praise to Me? Just try to imagine that.

The power of Creation would come alive. Its fruit would feed abundance to every corner of the world...so abundant that it would be free, for no amount of money could buy or store it. Praise produces tangible results, therefore, praise will always produce life. Stars would shine brighter, skies would be clearer, the earth would experience its pleasure, joy would abound, love would enrapture the world, and thanksgiving would permeate hearts.

This is My Kingdom.

You can bring it forth with the sound of praise.

Start in your own home. Your 'universe' will grow dramatically brighter, My Presence will fill your world, fruit will abound, and 'life' will come alive!"

BREATHE IN GOD

AS I FINISHED my prayer time this morning, this phrase popped into my mind:

"The number of my days will equal the number of my breaths." I just sat there and wondered. What could it mean? This is what followed:

"The number of your days will equal the number of your breaths." What do you think this means?

You can't live physically without the breath of air. Likewise, your spirit needs spiritual breath. How do you breathe spiritually? You take in all that is spirit."

"Unless you be born again, you cannot see the kingdom of God.' (John 3:3 NKJV) Being born again gives you new breath—but how do you breathe that breath in the spirit? You take in all spiritual things. Look up, look around, and look often. You will see all that I am.

For those who have eyes to see, you will find that what you see becomes a breath. I have breathed life into you, and that breath continues to bring you life. Some people develop breathing problems in the natural. Likewise, some develop breathing problems in the spirit. Take deep breaths that contain the knowledge and awareness of Me, My love, My glory, My power, and My presence in and around you. You will find that breathing Me in will become easier and your knowledge of Me will greatly increase. You will walk physically in the Spirit and move in My ways, not yours. You will find yourself thinking and being guided by My Spirit in situations that you would never have expected.

You must guard your eyes and let them focus on looking for My Presence, and unconsciously, you will be breathing Me in. Soon what you see will become such a part of you that being used by Me to bring blessings to others will become the 'natural' for you. And the number of your days will be filled with eternal things."

TREMBLE AT HIS WORD

"LET MY WORD penetrate your whole being. Let your heart tremble when you touch your Bible—'For it is alive, living, and active.' (Hebrews 4:12 ESV) Did you ever think of what that means? It has a life—a life of its own. It comes from the power of My being to create the anointed Word that is believed and spoken.

Don't just read words. Enter into its revelation. It means what it says—it speaks for Me. Your choice is to believe it and then act. You act by receiving it as if it were a weapon of mass destruction. It brings healing, light, and power, destroying the lies and darkness of the enemy.

Lay hands on the sick—power
Speak My wisdom—light
Listen with your spirit—revelation

I do not waste words. I used them to create the universe. Will I not use them to empower you to grow and become a power force from Heaven?

I am your Creator—ready to respond to the words you speak."

YOUR DOOR

I SAW A door open in the heavens. A single door. But as it opened, it was hinged to another and another and another—endlessly—causing the opening to look wider and wider.

The Lord said:

"Each door represents one of My children. The way I have made for them is open—this door is very personal. It is carefully crafted by My love and personal knowledge of each child. Everyone is joined together as it opens endlessly, but each individual is known and loved for his own quality and design. Your uniqueness is not lost in heaven but magnified.

My individual knowledge and relationship with you on earth doesn't change when you come to heaven. It is only enhanced by the reality of all you have believed.

Our joy will be full and is established for eternity.

Understand too, how painful it is for Me when those who choose not to come home...pray for the lost...they are meant to be family.

Look at the beauty and provision I have given you on earth. Would you ever be able to imagine such things? Yet they are only a vague representation of what awaits you here. I will be standing at the door—your door—when you arrive."

UNDERSTANDING

"WITH ANY HURT, there is an understanding that would heal it. You live in a hurting, confused world. There is the hurt that festers in memory and causes anger and unforgiveness. Then there's the hurt that opens the way to a deeper understanding of those involved by revealing the truth behind a remark or offense. It is almost always coming out of the experience in the offender's life. Realizing this and exposing that pain, brings understanding that also brings healing to both people. This heals the pain and deepens the relationship.

If these emotions weren't involved, you would never have true knowledge of a person. You would be like 'plastic people' making noise and motions that have no real meaning. Hearts wouldn't be involved. Hearts are the way to love and be loved. But when the heart is involved, so also is the possibility of hurt. Then, there is a choice. What is behind that hurting heart? Is it the offense or is it the buried hurt or unforgiveness in the person who is still unconsciously operating out of their past experience?

People hold grudges for years because they have no understanding. It could be healed in minutes, but one has to be willing to seek that understanding. You can be that person.

So why is all of this important? I want you to pray and look deeper into the people you know. You can bring healing in many ways. Don't live your life on the surface, go deeper. It is important that My Body functions in a healthy way. It can only do this by relationships based on truth and sincerity.

And if somebody hurts you—it usually has nothing to do with you. Look deeper."

ALONE IN A CROWD

"HOW IS IT that when you come into My Presence and we are alone together, so many others can come into My Presence as well—yet we are still alone?

As a child you were taught that I am everywhere. And I am. But part of that everywhere is with you. We have our intimate times when you are separated from all of your thoughts, activities, and duties, and I love those times. I love the chance to speak with you, share My love, and give you direction. I cherish the experience of revealing to you all that I have for you and how much I love you. But I want you to know that that experience is always available to you. I wait for you to come, to turn to Me and engage with Me all during your day—to talk with Me to share your thoughts, questions, thanksgiving, and love. Then, just rest with Me. You never have to leave, you can spend every hour here with Me, for we are of the same spirit, and you can go about your day and be with Me at the same time.

Don't separate yourself from Me by assigned times or places— but let the fullness of our relationship grow as you learn to breathe in My love even in your busyness.

Heaven is timeless. You can experience it now, and when the time comes for you to be in heaven, it will simply be a change in atmosphere. We will meet face-to-face, and we will fall into each other's arms as old friends who have spent a lifetime together."

THE DANGER OF STRIFE

"THE DANGER OF strife and its wounds. Strife is like a snake that snaps at your legs while you are trying to carry on your work. You accomplish your task but with the energy of the snipping serpent instead of the love that was originally intended for this work.

When you 'meditate' on this hurt or anger, you open the door to your heart. You allow this destructive force to accomplish its goal, which is to rob you of your joy and your strength and leave his poisonous wound instead.

Let Me help you know how to deal with this, for I know this thief well.

Do you remember the scene in the movie *The Passion of The Christ* in which the serpent slithered around My body in the garden as I prayed in anguish? I raised My leg and brought it down, stomping on the head of the enemy. I crushed him. There's your answer.

Get a picture of this in your mind, and the next time he comes trying to stir up ugly emotions, DO IT. STOMP ON HIM.

Do not let him play with your mind—do not entertain his thoughts. Recognize immediately whose they are. They are not you, for I have made you new. Don't let him invade you. Think of Me…sing to Me, and I will join you. I promise you, if you do this, the joy of My Presence will deliver you, and together we will sing and rejoice in your victory."

FINDING THE MYSTERIES

"A BOAT ON a blue lake. A few people in it. They float along enjoying the calm water, clear skies, and perfect temperature. It looks like a wonderful day. And it is—but is that all there is?

I have given you My Word. Some read it, some memorize it, some explain what it means to them, but they are all like the people on that lake. Most people just 'float on top' of the Word and take it at its superficial value. And that is good. You need to know what it says. But just as there are things deep within the lake, so there are much deeper riches in My Word. There are mysteries hidden there that you can can't imagine—understanding that will enrich your life and most importantly, bring you into a deeper knowledge and relationship with Me.

Make the Word like a 'belt of truth' that ties us together, receive it from My heart, for that is where it began. I will give you My Word daily as you need it because it's the source of My relationship with you. Communication is what brings us together. Let Me speak My Word to you. Some almost view reading My Word as homework and are eager to 'get it done.' But no, let it be your source of life. Let it work in you to develop our oneness. Let it become an experience with Me. That is why I gave it. Take the thought it shares, make it personal to your life, and let it convict, bless, teach, comfort, and entice you to see more. Put yourself in the place you are reading about and let its purpose reveal the love that teaches and touches you."

BREAKING THE ROCKS

"IS NOT MY Word like fire, says the LORD and like a hammer that breaks a rock in pieces?" (Jeremiah 23:29 NRSV)

"I am the Word, and there are rocks in you that have to be broken. Rocks of unbelief, fear, unforgiveness, and unwillingness. There are things I ask you to do that go against all of your self will.

I don't ask because it's easy. I ask because it's hard. They are the things you don't want to do. Things that would cause you to make really hard decisions against your own will.

What you don't know or realize is that these very things are going to bring you into a light so much greater than you can imagine. When that rock of resistance comes down, you will be standing in a new place—a higher place—and you will have drawn much closer to Me. This will not be because you 'earned it' but because you yourself have removed a barrier that holds you back. You will also find that suddenly you desire to do that thing which you were so opposed to.

The wall that stands between us is an unwilling heart. It becomes its own barrier that can only be removed by you. I have no power over your will. All I can do is offer My love to help you, and the moment you yield that rocky barrier to Me, is the moment you will see My glory in a new and increased freedom, giving you much greater light and revealing much more of My Kingdom."

APPRECIATE WHO YOU ARE

"A CIRCUS. ALWAYS in a circle. People watching. Both people and animals performing. Some better than others. But there is always that 'one' who stands out. However, no one who wants to see a circus, wants to see just that one thing.

It is the same with My children. There are those who are out front, doing or using their gifts. And then there are those who are the observers. They think of themselves as such because they don't realize their own gifts or purposes. They try to 'absorb' the Spirit by watching and listening, but they never appreciate who they are in this work of bringing My Word and salvation to the world.

I am going to sound the trumpet—it is time to rise up and be who you are, time to use what I have given you and do what I have called you to do.

Look to your heart. That is the engine of My Spirit. Obey its desires to serve Me. Let all else go. When you gave Me your heart, you gave Me the key to that engine. My Spirit will drive you to places you never expected. Go with Him. Don't let your gifts and holy desires lie dormant. Do you think that dream is just a dream? Or is it a vision? Don't be trapped by limiting the leading of the Spirit to spiritual things. I have given you natural gifts to be used in natural places to express and open the ways of My Spirit. Eternity will show the fruit of the smallest seeds. Do you see a ground where there is no growth and lies there empty? Then you are the one to plant the seeds—that's why you are there. Don't ever leave it empty. One day you will see a harvest you would never have imagined—a harvest that would not exist if you had not planted even the tiniest seeds wherever you went. You don't have to be an expert in memorizing the Word—just live it and share the truth that it contains."

THE ROCKING HORSE

"FAITH CAN BE like a rocking horse—it is never steady. It's fun but not supportive. You can hold onto it, but it has no sturdy foundation. Back and forth, back and forth, undecided, uncommitted but fun to play with.

This is how faith is to some—insecure in its foundation. To walk in faith you must walk on level ground, ground that never changes, moves, or fails to support you.

So, some see faith as a hope, while they fall weak on the inside and insecure in the outcome. Some see faith as an exercise, reciting the Word over and over. And again, some see faith as a firm confidence in the ground of our relationship. They are confident of My Word, My truth, and My promise, walking together, knowing My will, and ready to pronounce it. When you use My Word without that personal 'knowing' that comes by the Spirit, it falls into the hope category.

The Cross is the way to salvation, and yet not all receive it. It is not My Word of salvation that fails but a lack of knowledge of My goodness within the receiver. In the same way, it is not in an unanswered prayer, nor is it because of the person praying. In scripture, healing most often happened because the seeker went after it. Sometimes when you offer a prayer, the receiver is in a lower place of faith and can't accept a gift. But when the receiver is steadfast and ready to receive, he will."

WHO'S EATING THE MOST?

"WHICH MAN ARE you feeding? Your flesh or your inner man? The flesh will die, but the spirit will live. Where he lives depends on you. If you choose to live with Me, I will have a place prepared for you. I have given My life for this—to have you with Me. My greatest desire is for you to choose Me.

When you choose to turn from sin and give your heart to Me, My Holy Spirit comes to live in you and teach you My ways. This is called the 'rebirth.' This is your new inner man. The one who will live forever with Me. But while he's here, he needs to eat. He needs to be nourished. He needs bread—the bread of My Word. By this, he will become strong and ready to serve Me with power.

Then there is the flesh. The flesh just wants to feed itself. T man who is fed the most will grow the most. The value of that food will be reflected both by sight and by spirit. The only food the inner man needs is My Word—'I am the bread of life' (John 6:35 NASB) and will fill your spirit for all eternity.

Remember that there are little men in big bodies, and big men in smaller bodies. What you are on the outside does not reflect what is on the inside. How strong do you want to be? And which man are you giving your strength to?

Sit with Me. I will share My bread with you. Take your time, savor it, and let it energize you, let it cultivate a desire for more. Don't read it alone—read it with Me—cause your spirit to be aware of My Presence. Go slowly, don't rush. Even if your time is limited, go slowly and read less if necessary. You will digest it much better that way. Your inner man will grow stronger and stronger, and the world will soon become aware of your strength. Fed and nourished, this inner man will function and be known as a man of God."

CHANGE THAT TUNE!

"IT'S TIME TO change your 'tune.' Change your sound, your words, your rhythm— the way you pray. A new day is coming. Rejoice now for your Bridegroom is coming with power. Sing to the Lord, let your new song be filled with praise, with a new vibrant faith focused on Me, not the enemy.

It has been a long, cloudy day. Your faith has been weak, lit vaguely with the light of hope. You focus on the negative, now focus on Me and you will see Me in a new way. Lift up your heart and your face and you'll see and do things you would never have dreamed of. It is a time of war—but also a time of new weapons. As you trust Me, praise Me, and focus on Me, I will give you all that you need. I am a mighty warrior—I will rise up, and you will see My glory.

Be not afraid. Stand your ground and know that I stand with you. As the people of Israel watched their enemies coming to attack them, they set their faces toward Me and put their singers in front of their army to praise Me. I fought for them and gave them the victory. You will see Me fight for you as well. So sing a new song of faith, lift your eyes to Me, lead this war with your songs of praise, and I will do the battle."

THE FRUIT OF PRAISE

"PRAISE ISN'T JUST for Me—it is also My gift to you, for praise will bring you joy as well. We can rejoice together in the bond that praise brings. That is, praise from the heart—meaningful praise—not just a collection of words but thoughtful words declaring true thanksgiving for all you have, even unanswered prayers. Why? Because giving Me praise for unanswered prayer is one of the biggest gifts of trust you can give Me.

A child may not understand a good father—but he needs to trust him. So trust Me. I don't come in and out of your life—here, there, somewhere, sometimes. I am in you—I know all of your thoughts, desires, complaints, and worries. And I understand. I love you and want more for you than you can imagine. I am your Father. Trust Me. You know Me. You have repented of sin and invited Me to live in you. You have the teacher, My Holy Spirit, within you. What do you do next? Let My water cleanse you. Your life has been filled with words—from every direction. Teachers, parents, friends, neighbors…so there is much cleansing to do. Be washed by the truth and water of My Word.

Do you have thoughts or ideas that seem fine to the world but are contrary to the Word? Do you know the Word enough to even recognize the wrong?

Often people say that to relax, they need a nice long warm bath. That is what your spirit needs. A nice long soak in My Word. Do you have thoughts that draw you deeper into My truth? Do you listen to them and meditate on them? Do you agree that if you knew those thoughts were really My voice, you would respond differently? Well then, listen for that voice—and follow it. Let it wash you and your distant dreams and see how important you are to Me. There are dreams in you that are for eternity, and once realized, will last forever. Let My Word bring life to you and then share it. Do you look at the 'Book' of the Bible as living, active, and having power to work miracles? Do you contemplate the fact that one day, you will stand before that voice? I am your God, and I have a wonderful plan for you. Do you not want to hear it? You may see My Word as a list of rules and stories, but it is not—it is formed to speak to your heart, bring you life, acknowledge you as My greatest creation and the creation who one day, will rule and reign on My earth.

Do not limit your vision to your years here and now—but look to eternity to see who you want to be. Then act on it. I will meet you there."

FIND THE POWER OF MY WORD

"SOME QUOTE MY Word—but the truth is, that Word has not taken root. It is like the seed on the foot path. This failure is not because of a lack of truth but for the lack of faith and understanding.

So what is life? True abundant life is living in the reality and life-giving activity of the Word. It is not a hope, and it is not just for some—it is a command given but not received. What good is a Word that is not believed or received? What causes this lack? It is because of your eyesight. You see only the world you live in. You need to see My world and My perspective. How? By looking up and seeing

MY REALITY, and therefore, believing in and receiving My Presence. Think on that—look up and see the power that gives you life. THE POWER OF MY PRESENCE IN YOU.

This Word is not a belief system. It is a living and active relationship with the God who made you and designed everything in you. I know your needs—I know your deepest thoughts. And I want you to know Mine. Then take that reality and understand that I am in you as surely as creation is rooted in the earth.

Can you eat an orange off of a tree? Of course you can. Well I am 'Tree of Life'— 'eat' the truth from Me. I am in you, thinking with you. Absorb it—digest it and bear fruit. So don't just let it pass through your mental understanding—let it work to first bud, then blossom, and finally give you food to eat. Feed it to your body and address your needs. Others will see the Tree from which you eat, and you will become a branch that offers food, nutrients, and blessing."

WHO GETS TO EAT?

"YOU ARE SPIRIT, soul, and body. You must feed all three.

Your spirit needs the Word, prayer, and the power of My Presence.

Soul—read, look at, and enjoy good things. Whether it is in creation, invention, or entertainment—let it be spiritually healthy and it will unite with your spirit.

Body—eat what is good for you. Eat what I created, let your body absorb health, and then watch and be careful about what else you put in your mouth.

Exercise to move that health around your body. You will grow stronger in all three areas. You will feel well and balanced. Your strength and joy will increase. And you will be made whole."

ANOTHER WELLSPRING

THE WORD "WELLSPRING" came to my mind. I looked it up and it said, "original and bountiful source of something."

"I am your wellspring of life. What makes you think I will only speak to you when you are 'up?' Do you think I don't understand the moods of life?

Even when you are feeling sad—you are in tune with the wellspring in your spirit. Your mind and emotions won't always agree with the balance of peace in your spirit—but I do not separate Myself from you because a part of you is having a hard time. That's why I have given you the Comforter—because I understand, and I want to minister to your soul and bring it into peace with your spirit. Your body will automatically fall into its peace. Man's interpretation of Who I am can sometimes cause great confusion and turmoil if they seek and relate to Me by rules and not by love. Rules come out of love, but I want to bring you beyond that.

'Making love your greatest aim' (1 Corinthians 14:1-2 TLB) is not just something I ask of you—but something I do in My thoughts and hopes for you. My creation is born out of My love—and encompasses all parts of you. You don't come to Me in perfect condition—I come to you in your imperfect combination of emotions and through love, kindness, and understanding bring healing."

BABY STEPS ARE BIG STEPS

"BABY STEPS. A baby step is a very big step. For the first time, a baby is able to stand by himself. Until that time, he has had to be carried or wheeled, unable to be on his own. So this very first step is the beginning of a new life for him. He can go where he wants when he wants, and as his walking becomes strong and confident, he is on his way to independence.

But where will he go? What will guide him? Just like a traveler needs a map to direct his steps—so this baby needs a 'map' to direct his. The map I have prepared for him is My Word. It can give direction at any age, but when a person is nurtured by My Word at an early age, there will be fewer 'U-turns' and restarts to make.

You'll see that My Word is only activated by your faith. Your faith strengthens the use and ability of that Word to perform its work. That's why believing is so important. It releases the power held in the Word to fulfill its purpose. My words aren't given to read, entertain, or be limited to teaching. They carry a power to become what that Word says. That is why your faith and actions are needed to put it to work. Make use of it. Don't leave it on the page—believe it and receive its gift.

Leaving a hammer and a nail on the bench will not build a table.

So take My Word and put it to work. Add your faith and see what miracles you can build. If you believe, there is no ceiling or limit to what your heart is reaching for.

Those baby steps will lead to maturity as you learn to walk in My step."

A POOL IN THE GARDEN

"THERE IS A pool in the garden. It waits for you. When you come just to be with Me, worship wells up within you, and the blessing you intend for Me will rest on you.

As you pour your heart out to Me, it becomes a ministry to your heart. As you speak words of praise or thanksgiving, you experience My gratitude for you. You come to give—and you receive. You come to love, and you are loved. You come to sing, and I give you a song. The garden becomes a pool that reflects all that you give. It brings peace and healing. You are cleansed and restored. You leave vibrant and alive. How? Why? Because you have given your presence, love, and all that you are to Me, which in its very giving, returns to you."

THE ZEBRA

"A ZEBRA. PEOPLE ask, 'Do they have black stripes on a white body or white stripes on a black body? What do you think? And why the mystery?

Everything I made has a purpose and a lesson. Creation really does speak and instruct you, without words or sound. Watch, study, and listen—you will soon learn more than words can tell.

The zebra is a revelation of saving grace and truth. A black body with white stripes…there are some good external qualities in a man, but his core is sin and always will be. Therefore, a black body with white stripes. Unless…

It is reborn. Then it becomes a white body with black stripes. It has been born again and its core is now the purity of God. Still stained on the outside with sinful thoughts or deeds, but those will gradually be washed away. How do you tell the difference? Do you really need to know?

I am the judge. You are My witnesses. The light of My Holy Spirit within you will give you discernment when needed. All you need to be is the person who opens the door to My love. Be moved not by the stripes but by letting the light in your heart bring light to the dark, empty heart you meet as you speak of the love you've found. So enjoy and love the zebra—it is not yours to judge. It brings a message, but its mystery is Mine."

UPWARD HANDS

"WHAT DOES IT mean to you when you turn your hands upward to Me in prayer? Do you do it as a gesture or as an act of all-consuming surrender to Me—a surrender of trust?

Do you think that I pour out evil, or do you really understand and trust that I came to destroy the evil that assails you? I endured great evil in order to pour out goodness into your open and trusting hands.

When you are hesitant to trust Me, or think I would answer you with anything less than the great love that brought Me to the Cross, then you are limiting yourself to the deceit of evil and allowing it to do its work. Think of that—measure your faith by the trust you feel in your heart. IS IT AT PEACE? Can you truly say you have surrendered it to My goodness, or are there twinges of fear, unbelief, and/or confusion?

Open your hands to Me—lift them upward, and when you do, do it as an expression of faith, trust, and thanksgiving. Realize that your hands are helpless and empty—but Mine hold up the universe—and they will move powerfully to respond to your trust."

THE MAN IN THE STROLLER

I SAW A stroller being pushed, but the child kept growing to full size and yet still did not walk...

"All who come to Me are My children. But not all grow to full stature. Some are, even in adulthood, pushed and carried along by others, never realizing My personal call to them. This happens because those feeding them are not teaching them how to walk. They learn to depend on others, not realizing how special they are or how important they are to My body. Do I make men to be just a form? Empty of purpose? Of course not—My heart is to call these out of their strollers and into their individual purposes. Your faith in Me does not stop at just believing—you have much to offer the body, and it has great need of you.

Your gifts might not be 'religious'—they might be caring for others' needs, listening with your heart to offer help to those in pain, fixing something they need, driving them, caring for their children...these are all the inner organs, so to speak, of My body but so necessary...without them, the outer ministry would have no power. The needs and ministry are endless—but through all of it, share My love. Your testimony is your greatest strength because it is truth. It not only will bring them closer to Me, but it will come back to bring you life.

When you leave your seat at church, it's not over. It's only just begun. Develop one step at a time—realize that your dreams, desires, and abilities come from Me so what you become is your gift to Me. Fear not and don't be discouraged. To function as a whole, My Body needs every part—it can't function in a healthy way without you. I nudge you through the inspiration in your heart—look and listen to it."

IT'S ALL IN FAITH

"I FORMED EVERY inch of your body. I have a deep personal knowledge of all its needs. When it hears My Name and the power of My voice, it has to obey.

If someone offers to give you something you need and puts it on a table for you to pick up, it will only meet your need when you pick it up and use it. It is the same with healing. I have given you back the health that was stolen from you in the garden. I have restored all. Not just your heart and your soul, but your body as well. Why would you accept a partial salvation? Believe and receive the gift of My life. You don't need a lot of words just 'be healed,' 'be cleansed,' 'rise up,' 'be filled.' It is faith that heals, not just words alone. Faith declares the words that bring the promise, but without faith, the Word stands idle waiting to be used.

So, why you ask, is it sometimes so slow in coming? Some get healed in an instant. But for most, it is a process. Faith has wavered to unbelief—false teaching and a sense of hopelessness have invaded the truth, and it takes time and courage to rebuild.

But I have come that you might have life, and have it abundantly (John 10:10 KJV)—here and in eternity. But just as you gradually grow spiritually, you may need to grow in receiving. You received the Saving Word by faith, but you had no experience. Yet you were saved.

It is the same with your mind—it is gradually transformed as you walk with Me and become grounded in My Word.

And so it is with healing. Your body begins to 'wake up' and rise to My Word which has been forgotten for so long. But as your faith continues to grow, so will the activity of the Spirit be able to grow."

TRUE FREEDOM

"FREE. EVERYTHING I give you is free. Have you noticed that? Let's start with the air you breathe—it comes freely. Soil that gives life to feed you, rain that feeds the soil and cleanses the world, wind that brings refreshment, clouds that protect you from heat, trees that give you shade, sun that gives you light and warmth, a moon that gives you soothing light and helps you rest, music that stirs your inner being, grass that feeds the animals and keeps your ground clean, streams that keep fish fresh to eat, seas that can carry you around the world, stars that light the way of your heart, and all the found and unfound minerals in the earth. From the endless sky to the bottom of the earth, all is filled to meet your needs.

Above and amid it all is THE CROSS. The way back to Me. It too is free. You were deceived into sin. That cost you your eternal life. It separated us. But again, I gave you My greatest gift—Jesus—He died to pay the price to open the way back to Me and to restore the separation between us. You can live forever with Me for free—no charge. You can't earn this gift, and you can't buy it—you can only receive it.

You work hard to provide yourself with all the things you want. And you pay a dear price for that in many ways. But I offer you a wonderful, extravagant life in a world with never-ending love—for eternity—and it's free! Look around, take note of all that I have supplied for you—free. How then, after enjoying all I've given you, do you think you could possibly earn or pay your way into My eternal care? You have only to receive and say, 'Yes Father, I believe—forgive the sin that separates us—say yes Jesus, I receive your gift of life—yes Holy Spirit, fulfill in me the destiny of my Father.'

I give it all to You freely. You have only to believe and receive. Don't come to the gate and find that you don't have the price for entry.

Come to the gate and say, 'Jesus, thank You for paying the price for me, and giving me this gift of eternal life, at no cost to me but at every cost to You.'"

THE SHIELD

"A SHIELD. WHAT do you think? Most see it as a protection, and it is—there are fiery darts flying all over. But it is also an aggressive weapon. When you are protecting yourself from an attack, it lowers your strength and puts you on the defensive. But if you use the shield to move forward and repel those darts aggressively, it becomes a weapon.

Move forward while holding your shield high in front of you, repelling the attempts of the enemy. In doing so, you will become the aggressor and cause the enemy to back away. Fiery darts are sent to weaken you, hurt you, and prevent your ministry of love from doing its work. Defend yourself by giving and loving first, and you will disarm the weapon sent against you.

Love will always win. Even the work of the Cross is denied by unbelief, yet My love is always there to defeat the enemy's lies.

The enemy can only rob—he can't give or bless—so when you are weakened, look to see what has been stolen. Love, healing, trust, rest, ministry—these are the enemy's targets. So check yourself and see if any of these are weak and quickly raise your shield of faith, resist those darts, and look for a place to plant love. Do it quickly for it is your weapon. Don't let it become your wound.

Destroy the dart with love and you will prepare the way to the cross, and the enemy will lose yet another captive."

I SAW THE FLAG

I SAW OUR flag with diminishing stars until there were only the original 13.

"Every time you take a wrong turn, you have to go back to where you made that turn and make the right one. Everyone has made a wrong turn or wrong decision at some time—you usually wind up starting over, whether it's in a job, a relationship, a situation, or even one's education. But there is always a new beginning, a new hope or a new resolution. When that happens, go back to your origins.

The message of the flag isn't just for the country but also for individual lives. The same faith and fortitude shown in the foundation of your country can be applied to its people as well. The country is floundering because of individual choices, so only by individual choices can it be restored.

There will always be times when you will have to undo and redo until it brings you satisfaction. Think of the word...satisfaction. It brings peace, rest, and the inner pleasure of what you have done. But as hard as you try, it will only come as you ask yourself these questions: are you acting according to My nature or yours? Are you adding light to the world, the situation? Is it blessing people—both those you work with and those who watch you?

These are the things that will stand and influence others for good.

When evil opposes you, what do you do? Whose nature is revealed in your response? If you work to bring tranquility, it will always be with you. Everyone makes mistakes—not everyone cares enough to correct them, but the peacemaker does. Usually the term 'peacemaker' refers to one who makes peace with others. But it can also apply to making peace with yourself. 'Undo' the wrong and 'redo' the right, and you will always carry peace.

Share My love with those you meet and cause your country to be reborn"

THE BATTLEFIELD

"MY CHILD, YOU are not just in a war, but you are on the battlefield. Weapons are aimed at you from every direction. The enemy has weapons— you have My Word. Use it. Aim at the attack. My Word will bring peace and victory. It is truth that brings the confidence to stand on this field. The weapons formed against you are meant to discourage you, to keep you from believing and to keep you from fighting. They want to take you out and go onto another. Don't let them—stand strong on My Word, and I will restore you to an even higher place.

Don't fear or doubt, for these two are just weak weapons meant to weaken and destroy you.

Soldiers who go to war for their country don't blame the country for their wounds. But they come home victorious. So will you. David wasn't afraid of Goliath, and he only had a stone and a sling. That is a picture for you to see that it isn't the strength of the enemy but the power of My hand at work in My Word.

So set your face like flint as I did toward Jerusalem. Move forward to the cross. Place all the effects of those weapons there on the cross, and let them die. Evil will be defeated, and you will rise again, knowing more about how to fight this battle as you use your spirit to sling My Word."

THE LIFE IN MY WORD

LATELY I HAVE been very aware of how "alive" the living Word is. I was praying for a small Christian bookstore when I saw every letter, word and book, jumping as if to music. They were all so alive— they looked like an orchestra working together. Today I saw it again, in my Bible. God's Word is so active and ready to speak— its shout was like a song of praise. My hand shook as I laid it on my Bible—its life was overwhelming. When He says that it's alive, He means it!!!

Do you remember decades ago, there was some kind of children's character that was like a box or a book. When you opened it, it spoke, and if you closed it, it stopped. I think we do that with God's Word. It's always ready to speak, we just have to open it.

'Is not My word like fire,' declares the Lord, 'and a hammer that shatters the rock in pieces?' (Jeremiah 23:29 NASV 1995)

"I long to speak to My people. I love the times of worship and prayer. I love to hear your voice. But I also want you to hear <u>My</u> voice. To understand that I sent My Word to heal, speak, and give life to you. Don't let it be like a long love letter you never read. If you want to understand Me, if you want to experience My love, if you want to know how I feel about something, it's all there, waiting for you.

Imagine its miracle. It is the voice of your Creator, Lord, and God, hidden above all, at heights you can only imagine. My voice is breaking through and speaking to you personally. Sense the music as it flows through your heart when you read it. Let its powerful reality pound like a drum through your being. It is not just empty words on a page but the experience of My living reality aching to reach the ear and heart of My children. Touch it, feel its life, and feel My heartbeat on the page with excitement, knowing we are speaking together. Embrace My Word and you embrace Me."

EXERCISE IN THE WORD

I SAW A sailboat—small and with two sails—both with holes in them...

"How can the wind carry a boat if the sail allows the wind to go through it instead of guiding it? No matter which direction the wind comes from, the boat will just float along, going its own way. The power and direction from the wind can only carry the boat to its intended direction if the sails are solid and flexible, able to bend with the wind.

It is the same with My Word. You must be strong in the Word. It is so important to build your foundation on Me—on My Word—or you will flounder and float along in any direction. What you don't understand, ask Me, I am the truth, and I will always answer your questions. Holes can indicate confusion, wrong thinking, unbelief—any place where you are not confident of truth. You must discover and experience truth in your heart for yourself. You can't live on another person's experience. The strength and confidence you see in others are the same things I want for you.

You work out at the gym to strengthen your body. I have given you a portable gym—in My Word—rest your body and exercise your spirit in it. It cries out for food and strength. Build it up, fill the holes, and My Spirit will come with a mighty wind and take you to places you've never imagined."

YOUR NEW HEART

"LOVE YOURSELF AS I have loved you. I have given you a new heart—it is toward Me—that's all I ask for. All other things can be changed, but the new heart is My heart and will always lead you to Me.

People only have a change of heart when it is their own heart, still moved by sin, swaying to and fro by any inclination that moves them. It is weak, unsteady, much like the house built on sand.

But My heart lets you feel the love for others that I feel for you. Do not come into condemnation—that is a weapon of the thief—don't agree with him. Look what agreeing with him did to Adam and Eve.

Choose each day to agree with Me. If you know My Word, you will know My will, and you will always agree with righteousness. You can only do that by choosing to receive My heart. Then you will know My voice, My ways, and the path of righteousness."

LET MY LOVE INVADE YOU

"YOU HAVE COME to Me. I am yours. We are one. My being has made you. Just as a woman gives birth out of the function and nourishment of her body, so all things have been made through Me.

I did not fashion you out of dust that was idle and apart from Me but from the depths of My heart, compelled by the joy and love I had in creating you. If you only knew the tenderness and love I felt in forming you...there is no one like you.

So when you come to Me, it brings such joy—My heart is overwhelmed as we talk and share all that you want to be and all that I want for you. When you enter My presence with such love and humility, it opens the door to eternal blessings and the experience of glory that has no end.

Don't limit yourself—close your eyes, lift your head, and imagine Me, enraptured by joy in your coming. Stay and soak—let My love invade you, and draw you higher."

THE RAIN

"THE RAIN COMES and goes—and so with the wind. When it doesn't come, does it mean that the rain doesn't exist or that the wind has died?

So it is with people who don't believe because they don't see the evidence of My presence.

When you are moved in a relationship with Me, even the 'absence' becomes evidence of deep love and communication. A baby in his crib at night cries because he knows his parents are there and will come to his need. Then they leave, and he sleeps, knowing they are there, though not seen. And he is comforted.

So it is with us—I never leave you. But the wind and rain will not always be there. If it were, what need would there be for faith?

Faith is the root, the birth, and the life of our relationship. **See faith as a wedding ring.** It is a statement—and a loving reminder that touches your heart as you go through your day. **Declare your faith as you would your marriage** for I am your husband. I will never leave you or forsake you. You are Mine, and I want the world to know it."

THE CARRIAGE

"SIT WITH ME as in a slow moving carriage. Take time to take in the splendor of My world. I want to share it with you. Do you wonder how that beautiful flower was formed and how many different kinds and shapes and colors there are? Do you wonder how high the heavens are in the sky and how deep the hidden blessings in the earth? Do you wonder at the endless difference in trees and greenery? Do you wonder about the animals and how I feed them all? Do you wonder how only the soil can give life? And do you ever stop to think about how I created you?

You are like a well with things so deep in you that you miss them. What lies hidden in you? Is your life so filled with busyness and responsibility that you have no time to even notice the real you?

As you are taught to search the depths of My Word, search the depths in yourself. For it is My Word that spoke My purpose into you as I formed you with My own hands.

Just as all I created is according to My vision and purpose, I created you with a vision and purpose as well. As we slowly move along to study creation, envision what I have planned for you. If you miss the glory in creation, you will miss the glory in you. What makes you bloom? What gives you life? What makes you shine and cause people to see your beauty? It is there—trust Me—search yourself and your dreams. What brings you joy and pleasure? Do you love to love the unloved? To give, to help, to listen, to dance, to sing, to play music, to build, to create, to serve, to pray, to paint, to write, to minister, to preach, to understand…the list and desires are endless. You are not an idle creation, made to exist for a number of years and then come home to Me. You have a work to do that begins in your heart and goes on into eternity.

Look for life within you. It is My voice, spoken long ago when you were formed and born of My love."

MY WOUNDED TREES

TREES CUT DOWN, lying on the ground. The Lord asks…

"Who is cutting them down and why?

Do I give birth only to see what I have created destroyed?

As the 'religion' of the Pharisees and Sadducees killed My Son, so there are religions today that are destroying My Children who are hungry for growth and truth.

As the Pharisees and Sadducees added their own laws to Mine, I see the same thing happening today. Man dictates interpretation as gospel, people apply their own rules to fit their religious criteria. The health and life I created is often marred by man's design. My heart's cry is 'Come to Me,' give Me your heart, and I will fill it with My will and design for you. Don't make your own rules, just rest in My love and you will grow as the Cedars of Lebanon. Join with those who encourage My truth, not their own.

> Am I in the center?
> Is My power allowed to flow?
> Does My love flourish?
> Is My Word, My Word?

People move from church to church. They do this because they haven't found the life they are looking for. I have shown you My ways, don't add to them or take away from them.

Even the churches in scripture started to add their own rules—but I am the truth, the standard. Take My Word at its Word and you will find all you need."

FOREKNOWLEDGE

"FOREKNOWLEDGE CAN BE a dangerous thing. For then, all of your decisions are based on what you know. You become like a machine that operates according to a program.

Prefer mystery. There is no self-expression that is not discovered by experience. Learn from the process of discovery. All of life is a discovery. I didn't make pre-programmed robots. I made hearts that will dwell with Me and follow My lead. Hearts that will feel and learn and be soothed and know the experience of life.

Don't be afraid of life. Enjoy it. Use the capabilities I have given you to walk through it and grow through it. I am with you and hold you by your hand and will never let you go."

BLOOM LIKE THE FLOWERS

"COMING TO ME doesn't just mean you come in repentance for forgiveness of sin—it means to come with your whole being—your joys, hurts, pains, confusion…

When you come to Me, you come to experience understanding, healing, help, hope, and the power to overcome. You come to be refreshed by My love and will be restored in your soul.

Look at the wilting flowers. They respond so quickly to the slightest bit of water—hungry for more but encouraged by the knowledge that there is more to come.

I see both your joys and your pain—some seem to think I am only in the joy…but I am with you in your pain as well. I want to comfort you, heal you, and by understanding, lift you up, put you back on your feet, and restore your 'walk.

I will fill you with living water. Rest in Me. Rest heals your body but also heals your soul. Soon, like the flowers, you will bloom anew and enhance the beauty that surrounds you."

REAPING AND SOWING

I SAW A busy street filled with lights along the sidewalk. However, many of the stores were dark…

"You see the lights and the busyness, and you see the darkness. But do you see the people? They walk along oblivious to the dark stores and enter without any realization of where they are going. To them, there is no difference between light and darkness because they are blind. They move about without noticing the dangers that surround them. They eat, use, and wear anything that feels good. They satisfy everything but their deepest need—their hearts.

I am the light of the world, but they have no idea where or Who I am. That is, until My servants bring the light. Let this be a lesson to you. Just because they walk and talk with confidence doesn't mean they can see. They are still blind. Yes it is wonderful to bring sight to the blind eyes, but how much greater it is to bring sight to the blind heart. How do you do this? Draw them by love. When I said, 'Come follow Me' (Luke 18:22 ASV), 'Let your nets down' (Luke 5:4-11 ESV), 'I saw you under a tree' BSB) I was making it personal to them. Do this. When I spoke to the multitudes, I spoke to all because they all chose to come. I speak to hungry hearts. And the hungry will hear Me, for they know their need.

There are crowds of people in your life—how do you feed them? Don't let them be just one in a crowd…make it personal. Bring the light into their darkness. You may just be a seed along the way, but without you, they won't grow. Always be planting or reaping…always be ready and alert to the darkness in front of you—and always leave the light. Just show them My love by who you are and speak what I give you, and you will be either reaping or sowing. That is all I ask.

If the Spirit moves in you, speak it out—it will speak to their need. A simple, 'God loves you,' 'God hears you,' or 'God is with you,' is all it takes to open a heart. Speak it out and move on. I will do the rest."

STOP. LOOK. LISTEN

"YOU HAVE THE capacity to read the Word and never 'hear' what you are reading.

How much better to read a short sentence and really listen to what it says than to read a whole page and get nothing out of it. It is like eating two pieces of bread and calling it a sandwich, or eating just the skin of an apple, or just the pod that was holding the peas. Where is the filling, the nourishment?

Pray for ears to hear—to truly listen to the Word as it speaks to you. Open your heart and truly devote time to Me, without thinking of your own schedule. When you come to pray and read, come to Me—to My person— and hear what I have to say, personally, to you. Read slowly with your heart— don't just pass through it with your mind.

Read until you find life or a quickening. Then stop and listen. As you do this deliberately and train your spiritual senses, you will find yourself living it outside of the Word—carrying it into every aspect of your life. I am life, so when you find Me in the Word, you will also find Me everywhere because you are learning to live in Me.

Just enjoy My presence as I teach you and lead you into deeper understanding. Then, feed on it all day—let it fill you and nourish you instead of letting it sit on your brain and fade away.

I want you to know My love, not just your rules."

THE CRUMB

"DO YOU FINISH your plate when you eat? Do you enjoy every last bit of it? Or do you leave some on the plate and still leave satisfied?

Pay attention to this thought when you spend time with Me. There are times when you really are not satisfied, you're just ready to go on with other things.

I say this because there are times when I have things to tell you, but you leave before I can say them. Leave no 'crumbs' on the table that never get ingested—those crumbs may make all the difference.

One crumb can carry the way to a miracle. Don't leave until you feel the release, and know that you go with My blessing. I love our time together, and I want you to love it as well.

What is a crumb? Maybe a thought that will complete your understanding, a word that encourages you, a word to give you direction, a morsel of power that drives you with courage. Whatever it is, wait for it. I want us to share the deeper, more intimate things to bring us closer together."

THE DONKEY

"A DONKEY KICKING—IT is a defensive move. You too must kick against falsehood. Don't be afraid to counter every demonic lie with the truth.

Truth will always break through the confusion. Speak it in love or it will not be received. Soften the heart first—love is the greatest weapon. Speak with respect. But speak it earnestly.

Earnestness—a sincere attitude of truth for a loving reason. When truth is spoken out of sincere intensity, it will disarm an argument. To do this, you must know the truth. True knowing that cannot be disarmed comes from your experience. That is why you need time with Me. You need to know My reality and the heart of the Father. In that, is true earnestness. It is the reality of your experience not your belief system. You must know and speak for Me. Otherwise, it is just another argument.

You can build on your testimony by building on your experience with Me on a daily basis. My apostles just followed Me—they grew in their understanding by being with Me. There is no other way. You are My temple—keep building it, and people looking for Me will be able to come to you looking for direction. When you welcome them, you are inviting them into My temple."

Note from Pam:

I looked it up and thought it was interesting that horses kick and run. But donkeys kick and stand their ground!

APOSTASY

"THERE IS A great apostasy going on in America. In every area possible, there is a turning away from the worship and ways of God.

This will lead to a mighty outpouring of the Holy Spirit that will call the people back to Me and My grace. At the same time, there will be the force of judgment against all who turn away or deny Me. It is a spiritual war that will end in a victory for the country and a time of destruction for those who turn from the throne of grace.

For grace is given to all who seek Me. Those who do not turn to Me will experience a darkness they have never known. For I am the light of the world and without Me, there is no light.

Grace and forgiveness will always be offered—your destiny is always your choice for I died to save all. It is finished. You have only to say, 'Yes, Lord, I turn from my sins and receive Your saving grace.' Again, it is all and always your choice.

My heart breaks for those who choose darkness for they were formed and given life out of My love. I am not angry at their choice—I am sad. My heart aches and goes out to all who turn away, and it will never deny eternal life to those who come back to Me. I made them to enjoy My light, My life, and My love. But be aware—the day will come when it will be too late. Search your hearts now while the door is open…I see you and I wait for you."

ROMAN ARCHITECTURE

"COLUMNS—BIG STRONG ONES—LIKE in Roman architecture. It takes many of them to support the building and show its beauty.

Likewise, it takes every member of My body to support My Temple. If even one column is missing, it will not have full support or display its intended beauty.

Do you realize how important you are to My body? For I have made a place that only you can fill. No one can take your place, for My glory will only be fully revealed when My body is fully established.

Look to your own heart and desires—they will lead you to your place. Let no one 'assign' you your place according to their plan, but be obedient to the directions I have put in your heart.

Will the physical body be strong and healthy if the tiniest cells are not healthy? From where will it get its strength? The strong, muscular arm may give the appearance of strength, but if the supporting 'pillars' of cells are not equipped to do their job, the arm will be weak.

So then, the tiniest parts of the body give strength to the large outer 'limbs' so they can do their work. Do not take this lightly—for the whole body would not be able to function if every part was not doing its job. Don't judge and put your job on another person by thinking that your call is everyone's call—nor is their call yours. Both are necessary for My body to function."

THE BUS

"THERE IS A bus loaded with people. When they got on the bus, they chose the one that will take them where they want to go. They are all together headed toward the same destination. The bus will make stops along the way, letting people off and on at various places—however, it will not change its ultimate destination.

People influence other people—for good or for bad. Those who travel have made a decision of where they want to go. Are you on the right bus? If not, get off—easy as that.

People are enticed by what they see in others. Who do they want to follow? Which direction is right? If they are on the wrong bus, they can just get off at the next stop. But some don't even know where they want to go—they just know they want to get to the place where they feel at home and at peace, a place they never want to leave.

The question I have for you is, 'Are you on the right bus? Is it taking you where you want to go? Do people want to follow you? And, where will you lead them?'

Is the bus you are on leading you toward Me? Are you enticing others to join you in your travel? Everyone can change directions anytime they want to and keep trying different routes to different places, or they can get on My bus and just enjoy the ride, the joy, the activity, and My company.

I promise you, when you choose to go with Me, you will never want to get off. You have seen many people change different religions and churches. They just keep leaving, searching and leaving without even understanding what they are looking for. However, when they choose to 'ride' with Me, they never want to get off or change directions. They know they have found their destination.

If you are in a place that settles that search within you—where your heart is at perfect peace, where you have found your destination and know you are 'home'—then you are on the right bus. You will never want to get off, and it will bring you to the right destination—where you belong—home to My Father."

HERE COMES GOD'S GLORY!

"THE EARTH IS being filled with My glory. The earth has been groaning with hunger for this. Can you hear it? Can you see it? You are part of it. My glory is coming in power. The angels have been released and holiness is being poured into the earth. The riches of heaven's glory are beginning to flow, and there is no power that can oppose or prevent it. The door has been opened. Glory is coming.

Prepare yourself. Set aside all encumbrances and devote yourself to receiving all that is being given. You will be touched mentally, physically, and spiritually as the three disciples experienced on the mount.

The angels are filled with praise as they have waited for this moment— and so, they overflow with joy as a child does on Christmas morning!

Get ready and prepare yourself—open your clogged ears. Look up—for your salvation is drawing near. The devil runs in fear as the atmosphere is filled and flooded with My power. Did you know there is power in glory? Praise Me with the angels—join Me and you will never see fear again. I am coming."

TREMBLE AT THE SOUND

"DO YOU HEAR the thunder? Do you see the lightning? Do you recognize My power in it?

If you see it, if you hear it—I want you to imagine something else. Take what you feel when My power fills the skies—picture it—take in its power and glory...

Then try to imagine the explosive power at the birth of My creation! Power exploding at depths no one can conceive. An explosion that brought the mighty, glorious mountains, the deepest depths of the sea, the universe with forces no man can comprehend. Imagine it, hold it in your whole being.

Now compare it to the loving, gentle touch of My love as I created you. People stand in awe at the universe, and it is mighty. But how much greater is the power I have put in you? I have formed you by My own hands with the tenderness of My heart. I have given you power to create—to speak words and bring into being that which you cannot see. Good or evil, health or sickness, love or hate.

So, watch your words—they carry the power of creation. Watch your thoughts—words will follow. The only power you need is in My Word. Learn it, speak it, and hear it—you will see the light and hear it in the thunder."

MILITARY BATTLE

AS I SAT before the Lord, I was led to read excerpts from a booklet I received in the mail. It gave all of the real stories of persecution in the military, one in which they were forbidden to pray in the Name of Jesus outside of a chapel. They are being court-martialed, forced to resign, accused of treason, committing acts of spiritual rape and declaring they are enemies of the Constitution. One Marine was even court-martialed for having a scripture written on a piece of paper on her desk. Her supervisor took the paper and threw it in the trash. When I finished reading, I couldn't imagine what the Lord was saying.

Then I heard this childlike story.

"The little mouse stood straight and confident as if he were in charge of the world. The giraffe stood tall and strong with a chest of iron—he could see for miles—and alert all the others to the dangers coming their way.

The squeaky little mouse shouted his orders but could not be heard for its weakness. 'Shut the mouth of that giant he shouted—he must submit to me. He must only speak my words and do as I command.'

The command was given, but the giant giraffe didn't respond as ordered. He did, however, praise his Lord, Jesus Christ, with all of his mighty strength and sound. He started shouting orders to the mouse—the authority of Jesus caused the mouse to shrink and become unable to speak any commands. The voice of Jesus drains all power and ability to accomplish evil's call.

Time went on and many voices were agreeing with everything Jesus said, and the constant echo of His voice gave strength and size to the followers of Jesus. While the mouse decreased in size and strength, the giraffe grew in stature and might. When the world had reached its end—Jesus brought His children home and the door was closed.

Those who chose to follow the mouse found themselves disillusioned, powerless, and living in an eternity of darkness. Those who found the 'Light of the world,' (John 8:12 ESV) would never see darkness again."

The little mouse is the devil who is standing against God. The giraffe is a picture of true military strength given to those who stand for the Lord in the middle of spiritual battle.

FROM BELIEVING TO KNOWING

"THE DRUMS ARE starting to roll, the light is getting brighter in the Spirit, while darkness increases on the earth.

The darkness is beginning to shudder for fear of the light. Lies, threats, and hidden agendas are being revealed. Darkness cannot live in the light, so every day, pray for light to increase in you and in your world.

Step back and search yourself. What part of you is truly illuminated? What part of your faith would you die for? Do you have to keep 'turning on the switch,' or has it truly found its home in your spirit? How easily can you dispel the darkness?

Only as you walk with Me, as you pour out your heart, your questions, fears, and doubts, will all doors open to an understanding of truth. Don't develop a mindset—come closer. Come deeper by simply being honest about the truth you feel. You will experience true grace to help you **know** what you now only believe.

Would you rather read a book and leave it all on the page, or would you rather 'live' the book and simply become a living copy?"

GOD IS MY MAKER

"WHEN YOU LOOK at a seed or a bud, you know that Life is there and that what you see now is far different from what it will look like when it comes into full bloom.

And so, just as you wait and watch it change its form, it only hints at what it will be. In the same way, I wait and watch for you. The difference? I see the finished product, you don't. That's why you get down or displeased with yourself—because you think that you are finished when you are only just reborn. You are really only at the beginning. Did you ever contemplate growth? It takes time and can be very slow. The beautiful petals on a flower don't appear at the beginning, but oh, when they do…you stand speechless before their glory. And then, filled with this glory, they are seen and enjoyed while people marvel at this new creation.

As you see them, I see you, still changing and moving closer every day to the vision I hold for you.

Be still and know I am God (Psalm 46:10 ASV) You need to rest in My faithfulness to bring you through. Do not focus on the seed or the bud, I have only just begun to bring you into full bloom. But then, at that moment, you will see and say, 'Praise You, Father for Your faithfulness in making me into what you want me to be.'"

THE UNITY IN MY PRESENCE

"YOU NEVER WALK alone, you have chosen to walk with Me.

Everyone is walking at different paces—and for different purposes. Some are ahead, some are behind, but all are moving toward the same place.

When you joined Me in My walk, you started following My footsteps. You were trying to be obedient, failing at times because of fleshly desires, emotions, and selfishness. I picked you up and we continued on. You learned obedience gradually, although not perfectly.

Finally, we reached a place where your understanding grew to find something unexpected—something that drew us closer together—we are a team. Now, we walk together with the same intent, purpose, and determination. All along we moved together, but now it becomes something more. You walk WITH Me as a partner. We need to be intent on the same things at the same time. To share the same vision that is born in the same heart. No more running ahead or falling behind. You will find both peace and rest in sharing our stride. This will come from spending time with Me, being filled with My Presence, and sensing My Spirit. No more checking, struggling to keep the pace, unsure of when to go or how to get there. If you walk in My presence, your stride will come naturally and you will find rest even as we increase the pace or slow it down. In this is our unity."

THE WILES OF THE MOUSE

"A MOUSE EATING cheese. The cheese is filled with nutrition. The mouse feeds on it not just to fill himself but also to rob the cheese. He will keep on eating until there is nothing left and he has fed himself and robbed the goodness that was there.

This is what the devil does. He 'chews' at you to deplete the good and leave his mark. His goal is to leave 'scars' that will become roadblocks to your growth. Scars become like hardened ridges that create barriers between your heart and Mine.

Of all the lies and deceptions he uses, if you look closely, you'll see that his primary work is to rob you of My love and then leave his lie to continue the assault.

Learn to recognize his work and quickly turn to Me. If repentance is needed, do it and move on. My promise is to restore your health and heal all your wounds. Resist him, he will flee, and I will cleanse the debris.

Remember, if correction is needed it will come with love. If it's a constant degrading accusation, recognize it and turn from it—don't let him chew."

THE ZEBRA EXPOSED

I SAW THE zebra again...this time, all stripes were removed.

"The day has come when the zebra will be all white or all black. It is not for you to judge, but it will be clearly seen in the times ahead. Evil used to be known by its opposition to My Word. Now, the measuring stick has been removed—anything is acceptable. Hatred and injustice are the weapons forged against righteousness. Evil is called good, and good is called evil.

To the righteous, it is clearly seen. To the wicked, it is a time of freedom where evil itself can rule and reign in the world and in man.

They think they have obtained an uncharted release from restrictions and responsibility. This is called 'lawlessness.' As a result, we can now see clearly that the zebra has lost its stripes and its colors are revealed.

Why am I telling you this? Because revelation is just that—revelation of all things—nothing hidden. But evil is so clearly revealed that even some of the most unbelieving hearts will turn against it.

There are times when the revelation of evil is the only way to a person's salvation. And when that revelation of darkness becomes real and personal, My glory becomes a power—a power released into the formally closed heart and mind. Good will always triumph over evil, but it cannot triumph until evil is exposed.

So be at peace—I have not left you in this battle alone. I am your refuge—I am your Lord, your God—and I am your Father."

THE OLD MAN DIES

"WHY IS THE 'Old Man' in you called the Old Man? Because he is as old as the world. He is the 'sin nature' that goes back to the very beginning of sin—back to the garden. His nature runs loose and free, following its every desire, causing a wall of separation between My children and I. This nature is born in and rules every human being, making sin the natural course of life.

The penalty for sin is death, thereby making eternal death the only direction it can take. Since every human being is born with this sin nature, the old man thought he ruled a kingdom—a kingdom of darkness. If every man sinned, who could pay the price for sin and set them free from it?

But this old man forgot about MY nature. And that is to save MY children! So I took on the body of man in Jesus, paid the price for sin by dying on the cross, and then, to this old man's surprise, I rose from the dead! With joy in the truth that I have destroyed this separation, I can now welcome all who would come to Me. I have made the way for you—as you come, I will give you a new nature—My nature—to both reveal My love and change your desires. You will be set free from your sinful heritage, your old man has died, and you are born all over again. Will you be instantly perfect? No.

The difference is:

1. You will repent quickly when you make the wrong choice and experience the healing of repentance.
2. You will no longer have a love for the things you turned away from, they will no longer satisfy or excite you. And if you fall into them again, you will find you have a new disdain for them.
3. Now you know your destiny. You are anointed, sealed, and filled with the Holy Spirit, giving you a new heart and the promise of what is to come.
    You have already passed from death to life and have your security set in Heaven.
4. You will discover things about yourself and the gifts necessary to serve Me. You now have eternal purpose."

THE TROLLEY ON THE MOUNTAIN

"DO YOU KNOW there is a call on your life? You have a purpose to fulfill. There are those among the faithful who spend their time 'riding a trolley' around the bottom of the mountain. They believe in Me but have found safety and comfort resting in the pews and being fed. It is good—but don't confine the journey to the the rails. Make room for personal discovery and inner revelation.

Then there are those who do venture further—they set their hearts and climb a spiritual mountain. This takes a lifetime. This mountain echoes My voice as it reverberates with the sound of My Presence. My words come not by mouth but by experience, and My power brings you to your knees.

No one can teach experience. You have to make the journey yourself. This climb brings us together in a deep and personal way, unique to each of My children and their call.

It takes time for you to get to know Me. Personal time. Prepare yourself to meet with Me each day. Time to pray and seek Me in your own words with a hungry heart. Time to hear Me through My Word, and time to let Me minister to you.

The more you seek, the higher you will go. The higher you go, the more you will understand. The more you understand, the more you will see. As you gaze from the heights, the clouds of confusion leave and clarity will guide you even higher.

My call goes out to everyone. Don't settle, reach out, climb the mountain, and you will experience Heaven's glory—and your call."

TAKE THAT FIRST STEP.

"LISTEN. I HAVE something to say to you…

Put one foot forward, then another. One step at a time. I will lead you. You have only to obey—one foot—then another.

I am not talking about small physical steps, but a listening ear and an obedient response. Let this response be without adding your assessment or understanding. Just one foot, one move as you hear My voice or feel My leading.

It is just like when I speak to you. I give you a word or a picture, and the rest doesn't follow until you write that first word. You step out in faith and I move.

It is this first step that opens the way to increased light. Don't hold back until you think you understand the whole plan—just relax in the Spirit and let Him move you without your understanding, without your input. Just 'float' in Him as you would in the water, and He will be the current.

If I showed you the whole plan, you immediately would begin using it to make your plan—adding, deleting, rearranging. All this needless mental chatter will only add great confusion to My plan. Were you there when I created the universe? No? Well, look—it works!

Trust Me. One step at a time. When you learn to do this, you will find yourself in spiritual places you have never imagined, doing things you would never have dreamed of. One step at a time."

LIGHT BRINGS UNDERSTANDING

"AND GOD SAID, 'Let there be light' (Genesis 1:1 KJV)—and there was light. Then God made two great lights—the larger one to govern the day, and the smaller one to govern the night. He also made the stars. (Gen.1:16 NLT)

Things are harder to see and find in the dark. But that doesn't mean they're not there. When the light comes, you think that's all the light there is—until a brighter light comes.

That is why some use the expression, 'I see the light' when they suddenly understand something they have been struggling with.

Then there are those who live in the light but don't understand that there is more. Some have lamps in their homes that, with the turn of a switch, can increase the light, making it brighter and brighter. Just know there is always more.

Don't ever be satisfied. Always look for more light, more wisdom, more in our relationship. Don't get a glimpse of light and stay there.

Don't be afraid to seek more of My Presence, in doing so, you will find more of all you seek. There are things hidden in the darkness that will bring greater light to your understanding. When you seek Me, seek also those hidden things that I want to share with you.

Darkness doesn't mean it's empty—it just conceals the things we don't understand.

Don't think that because you have come to the end of your understanding, that there is nothing else there. There is always more!"

WHERE IS MY GLORY

"MY GLORY IS in you—but you cover it with unbelief. You hide it under the cloud of unworthiness. Understand this—no one is worthy! If I waited for all to become worthy, I still would not have been born into this world. I came to an unworthy world by the anguish of My unfailing love for you. And still, by questioning that love, you deny the experience of it.

There is a superficial assent to what I have done that fills My body. No one knows the depths of My heart—if they did, My people would shine like the sun.

As it is, you are like the moon that dims behind a cloud. Not because of the prevalence of sin but because of your own belief in the depths of what I have done. If you truly knew this, you would find the joy that is crying to come out.

The Cross has become a symbol of a belief system rather than the anguish of My flesh poured out for the world.

Throw away that unbelief—face your unworthiness—then together we can truly rejoice in your salvation. All of your sin and unworthiness has been dealt with. You repented and turned from it, yes, but to whom did you turn? Did you turn to a self-inflicted lifestyle of holiness or to Me and the glory that is revealed in the repentant heart that rests in My love?"

HIS SCARRED FEET

AS MY HEAD was bowed in prayer, I saw the Lord's nail-pierced feet right before me. They were so close and so real.

Then...

"My feet have walked the path of suffering and joy. The joy of doing My Father's will is the greatest joy in the world. The piercing, the pain cannot compare. I carry the scars as a reminder of what that pain has accomplished— and they are scars of joy.

Knowing that I have made the pathway open for you to come to your Father is an ever present gift both for Me and for you.

In this world, suffering will come. The devil thinks he can destroy your faith and trust by bringing about such pain, but...let My scarred feet be as the sound of thunder treading on the works of the devil.

The price has been paid, his battle is lost. So when you are in need, focus on My feet and the path that I walked. Listen and hear the thunder—and know your enemy is defeated."

COMING INTO HOLINESS

"I CAME TO cleanse you and bring you to holiness. My Holy Spirit uses My Word to wash you from the stains of the world. The speed with which He works depends on how often he has the opportunity to use the Word.

Get serious with the Word—don't read it to get through it or to accomplish some reading plan. Put yourself in it. Imagine yourself as if you were the only one I am speaking to. Separate your mind from it and read it with your heart. That is where the cleansing takes place, and then your mind will gain in understanding.

Your mind cannot be truly renewed without a change in the heart, so let your heart listen. Bring your mind into subjection to the spirit, and holiness will begin to grow and become visible naturally.

And then the day will come when you stand before Me cleansed, filled with joy, and ready to start your new life with Me as I originally planned."

JUDGING YOUR FAITH

"PRAYING IN FAITH carries authority on its own. The power is in the faith. That's why I gave it to you. It just happens automatically because the power is there when you believe.

Praying in hope has no authority and it decreases the power in the prayer. However, when you pray in hope, it is better than not praying. I bend low to hear you as you would bend to help a toddler trying to walk. I lead you on toward faith, and like exercised muscles, faith will grow.

Getting into the habit of prayer and expectation empowers your belief system. Praise and thanksgiving will increase results and will help your faith to grow.

Being faithful to pray is like being in labor. The baby will be born and grow to be a strong vessel. So as you seek Me in faith, I will hear you and will work to bring you to a place where faith comes to full term. Little children believe everything you tell them—they soak it in and receive it as truth. Be like them. Watch them, learn from them. Be earnest, hungry, and believing.

Do you want to know where your faith is? Here is a test that will help you find your way...

Do you believe the ground you walk on is solid and able to support you and all you have? Do you ever doubt it will hold you up? In the same way, do you believe I want to heal you and use you to heal others? Examine your feelings. There is your answer."

SHEARING THE SHEEP

I SAW A sheep partially sheared—like in circular patches. So I looked up the purpose of shearing. It has three purposes: to get the wool, to protect the sheep from the gathering of parasites, and to cool them off. I asked the Lord about it and this is what He said:

"My people are like a partially sheared sheep. Shearing is a process in growth.

Parasites—these are things that cause, anger, unforgiveness, or harm to you in any way. This shearing is best for cleansing and healing.

To Cool—this shearing gives you peace. It removes your burdens, worries, sickness, fears, and negative thinking.

Wool—these are the things in you that I use to bless others and to bring healing, encouragement, love, supply, and understanding.

Shearing is an example of the process you are in. It takes time, but as long as you submit to the shearing, you can rest knowing that you can trust My hand. Obedience and cooperation with the move of the Spirit will bring about a perfect sheep, so don't be impatient with yourself, don't deride yourself, just rest and trust My ways, and My love will be at work in you.

As you see Me work in others, support and encourage them with the same patience I show you."

WHAT IS MY LIFE?

"MY LIFE CARRIES My Presence—My Presence carries My truth—Truth carries fulfillment of My will.

The only way into life is in and through Jesus. Many look to be satisfied with worldly things, but those things don't last and will only satisfy a small part of that person. Becoming whole can only happen in Me.

That's why there are so many factions, all trying to satisfy the very basic need that they were made for—a relationship with Me. It's like somebody trying to duplicate something I have made—it's only a counterfeit with no life of its own.

Life without Me is always going to be a counterfeit. It's not real, it is manufactured. True life is fulfillment—life on your own only resembles life and is always in the flesh. It does not satisfy the inner being. You are spirit, soul, and body. The counterfeit will operate in only one area, it will never operate in its full potential. A spirit set on a false spirit, a soul set on meeting all of its own desires, a body that is in great shape but barren in the fullness of life.

I created you to be filled with purpose, vision, and the gift of representing your Creator. Only then will you carry My Presence and life. Only then will you be filled with peace and potential, growing into your eternal purpose."

STANDING IN HIS PRESENCE

"WHEN YOU HAVE finished everything you have to say in your prayer time, when your thoughts are finished, and when you are able to listen for My voice, stand silent in My presence. What do you hear? What do you think? Bow your head and let everything flow out and away from you—become empty.

Surrender all of your worries, fears, pleasures, and hopes—let them pour out. Can you feel it? Now, let your will leave too.

How do you feel? Are you beginning to feel surrendered? That's what I want. Surrender—give it up. Don't worry—I will always be with you. Don't fear—I am your shield, I am your blessings, and your hopes are in My hand.

The best place you can be is right here—emptied of yourself and ready to be filled with the power of the Holy Spirit.

Living waters will cleanse you and make you fresh—they will restore your energy and your resolve to serve Me. Close your eyes. Do you feel the purity of the water as it cleanses you? Be still. Don't think—just let it happen. Do you feel life starting to fill you? Is peace becoming joy? Soak in it. Stay a while. When you come to this place in prayer, vision and purpose will begin to come alive and I will speak to you. Listen to your heart.

As you leave, watch for the opposition. Whatever opposes love—it's not Me. Whatever opposes forgiveness—it's not Me. Pay attention to where your thoughts come from. If they are from your mind, who or what is influencing your thinking? Is it My Word or the enemy's? If you follow this rule, your peace will go with you."

TAKE SHELTER

"LEARN TO LISTEN to My heart. Look deep within you and you will find it. All of the idle confusing thoughts flowing through you are just disruptions trying to 'deafen' you from hearing My voice, robbing you of the truth you are experiencing. The devil is trying to place his thoughts, sin, and complaints on you.

Don't accept them. They are like birds flying overhead, leaving their droppings on you. But I cover you and protect you. You can't stop their 'rain,' but you can take shelter from them.

I am your shelter, your sanctuary. So again, you will find that shelter by looking at the depths of your heart—where I dwell. Deep down, you know the truth of My love and My understanding. I see the battle that comes against you. Don't join it—send it away and come back to peace.

I know you're not perfect. That's why I came. Accept that and follow My Spirit—not the birds."

THE MESSAGE OF THE CROSS

I SAW TWO hearts beating—at conflicting times. Then, there were many hearts, all beating to their own rhythm…

"All of these hearts belong to Me—but not all are in sync. Each does its own work, and it is good and I bless it.

However, the goal and vision is for each heart to beat and be in rhythm with Mine. Then we would be one heart—together.

How can this happen? By dedicating your own ways to Me. Move IN Me, not just on your own.

You have heard the saying, 'Everyone marches to his own drummer.' That is good and designed by Me as it applies to the different calls on each of your lives. But the heartbeat of those calls is the foundation of My love. I want My body to exhibit My love, together. Yes, you have doctrinal differences, but don't bring them before the world, with your disagreements shattering the purpose of the Cross.

My death and Resurrection were not to 'win an argument' but to save the lost. And that will only happen as you bring My love and healing to those who are suffering the separation from Me, no matter how it is expressed.

Pray for healing in the Body and wisdom to bring it together.

Let the earth be filled with one Mighty Heartbeat of life, love, and forgiveness. Let the message of My heart on the Cross be realized in the oneness of My children, expressing the power of having been forgiven."

THE LORD'S WEAPON

SEARCH YOURSELF. FIND your weaknesses. Then determine to search out My Word for the Word that addresses your particular weakness or problem. Then, use it as a weapon—smashing that stubborn weakness with My Word. It will destroy what it is aimed at. Don't use it or take it lightly and then go on—shatter it, and replace it with the fruit of My Word.

Don't dwell on your failures—dwell on My victory over them and then receive it. It's already done. Move on and get past all the negatives—learn to receive what I say and then do what I tell you to do. You will rise up out of the debris praising Me.

At My death, the earth shook and quaked—its sound roared through the earth. The skies were filled with My power. At this moment, I, the living Word, shattered all lies and darkness. It was done. Yet the devil still tries to use it. Don't let him lie to you—you know the truth. Let it set you free. The choice is yours—determine to rise from the darkness and live in the light."

THE POWER OF THE INNER LIFE

"MY LIGHT HAS come into your life. And so, you 'walk by sight' through the things of the Spirit.

What is this thing that has happened to you?

The Word comes alive and speaks to you, your heart responds to My voice and My touch, your spirit sees things others can't imagine. My life gives you joy and energy, visions call you forward while My Spirit gives you strength and courage. There is a whole new kind of life that no one else can see or experience without My light.

Not only does My Spirit bring the ability to see what is beyond, but to see a revelation of a whole world apart from the earthly flesh. It's a revelelation of a life still contained within you but as endless as the eternal universe. How exciting My world is and how excited I am to have you in it. Don't shy away, come forward with arms outstretched and say, I am here and I am ready, Lord!"

WATERING THE KINGDOM

"TO FIND WATER you have to dig. The water is there, but you have to go after it.

It is the same in our relationship. Some settle for the first sign of water and drink at the same depth every day—or every other day or every week.

How thirsty are you? Do you drink every day, and do you dig to go deeper? Do you have a thirst that draws your whole being into that well? Do you thirst so much that you want to get in and soak your whole being in its water?

Seek and you will find. But if you stay idle or are satisfied, that is all you will get. So dig, thirst, swallow as much as you want—guard against being satisfied, for in Me there is no end.

Every day meditate and absorb what you have received that day until it is part of your every cell. You won't have to memorize it, it will become an experience that you will never forget. Bathe in it all day, and it will replace the old and become a new part of who you are.

This water is the life you give to your new inner man. It brings light, wisdom, and illumination to the ways of My kingdom within you.

Come every day and draw from My well. Let it cleanse and refresh you, replacing the old and lighting a fire in the new."

LET THE SPIRIT SEARCH YOU

"THERE ARE THOSE who sit by My pool and rest but never go in. They enjoy My Presence and the warmth of the 'Son' but never enter the water of the Holy Spirit. So I give you an invitation to My pool—I have prepared it for you—come, swim in My water. Ask for the power of My Holy Spirit to bring you in. It is anointed to refresh, enlighten, instruct, and empower you. You will be bathed in truth and goodness and anointed to share it.

As you swim, you will learn how to exercise and use spiritual muscles you didn't even know you had. You will be strengthened with the power that enables you to run the race and bring many with you. You will know and experience My heart giving you wisdom, kindness, and understanding. These things seem small and frail to the world, but in the Kingdom of God they are power.

There is always more available to you, there is no end to the supply in My Kingdom. So look within you—there is no limit to what you can see. Let My Spirit search and reveal to you all that is in you, and you will find a spiritual life you never imagined."

UNDERSTANDING IS THE KEY

"CLOSE YOUR EYES. Focus on the fact that I am in you and surround you with My Presence. 'In Me, you live and move and have your very being.' (Acts 17:28 KJV) We are one. I hear every thought, prayer, and regret that come from your heart. I not only know, I understand.

Think of that word - understanding. It is the key to all and in all relationships. It is a melting pot for love. It is the joining not just of minds but of hearts. It is the door to deeper relationships., Before you judge, try understanding. You will find that it is this, that gives birth to forgiveness."

USING THE ARMOR

"CAN YOU SEE a soldier in full armor? The armor is strong and solid, but pieces of it keep slipping off. Much time is spent picking it up and putting it back on. The soldier tries to attach one piece of armor to another, trying to hold it all together and keep it from falling off. But each piece of armor must be able to stand on its own. It must be secure in its purpose and able to function as needed.

In most cases, the armor is too big—you have to grow into it. And you will grow into different parts at different times. When something is too big, you have to hold it up or it will fall off. But when it fits, it will hold its own.

You will find your armor fits better and better as you use it and as your inner strength begins to fill it up.

Don't give up, just use each piece as it becomes necessary, and gradually, you will find yourself proficient at using that sword of faith, filling those shoes with peace, and knowing Whose you are.

If I live in you, if you believe in Me, if you know My Word and My promises, and if you trust Me, you will have all the armor you need."

THE CAMELS

I SAW TWO camels—with a caravan following in a cloudy distance.

I heard…

"Most people see camels as interesting, but there is no cuddly attraction to them, so to speak. They look proud and even arrogant and are really just confident of My care and are at peace.

So what does that have to do with you?"

I said, "Lord I don't know anything about camels," and then I couldn't help but look it up.

Google said that they have one or two humps in which they carry fat that becomes an additional source of their food supply. humps also help insulate them against the intense heat in the desert.

He went on: "You need to do the same thing. Have an ongoing abundance of My Word hidden within you. That Word will insulate you against the 'heat' of the hour on the earth.

Do not be moved or discouraged by what you see. Feed on My word, build up your food supply, and you will be cool and at peace in the 'heat' of this day.

Have the confidence of the camel, don't focus on the evil. But know that I have overcome the world. Truly learn to live and move and let your whole being be at rest. Let what appears to be arrogance, be a solid confidence in Me."

GRASPING MY PRESENCE

"THE WONDER OF My Presence. Do you really take this seriously? Is it possible for anyone to truly enter into this reality?

God and man. I am God, and I am in you.

Meditate on that over and over, and let it go deeper and deeper.

I, Creator of the universe that you see with your eyes, the One Who fashioned its decor and empowered all power, live in you.

This is the cornerstone of your faith. This is what will move mountains. This is what you sense but cannot seem to reach. The more you ponder the revelation of this truth in you, the more power will be heard in your prayers, the intensity of your faith will produce miracles, and My Presence in you will take on dimensions you cannot describe.

Close your eyes, bow your head, and feel the weight of My glory that dwells in you."

LET THE UNIVERSE BLESS YOU

"YOU WILL NEVER be without lights, but there are times of greater light and then there are times of less illumination. Look at the sun, the moon, and the stars. Take joy in them all. They all have a purpose.

There are times in your life when you will see more clearly than at other moments. All of these times fit into different seasons of your life.

Spiritually speaking, compare these to those times you feel you are hearing from Me in very clear ways—it is all as bright as the sun. You have no doubt it is My voice—you see clearly and understand what I am saying to you.

Other times it seems you have to 'reach' to hear Me or to understand, and there are times when understanding doesn't come at all. You don't have enough light in the darkness to see clearly but enough to know that I am with you.

Finally, there are those times when it seems dark, but there are little touches of My love that sparkle around you, reminding you that I am with you and will help you.

These might seem to you to be just parts of your daily world, but if you will receive them, they can each touch you with the intimate understanding that I am with you, I am pleased with you, and I am at work in what you are doing in your life.

Look up—take in My Universe and enjoy My creation as it speaks to you. And remember, I am as present in it all as I am in you."

A LIVING HEART

"PICTURE A HEART. See it as a place of storage. As you read My Word, do it slowly, making each central point a <u>picture.</u> As the words form the picture, your heart will receive it. You will not have to struggle to remember it, for it will be like calling forth a memory rather than concentrating on the correct form of words.

When you form a picture, your meditation on that word will also cause you to be aware of My Presence in that word. Then that word will become an experience. This experience will present itself as understanding.

That is why My Word is called living and active. It creates, it has power, and when it is birthed in your heart, it will not be forgotten."

THE LAUNDRY BAG

"DIRTY LAUNDRY IN a bag. Everyone has some. Deeds, memories, actions against another, emotional scars, physical abuse, mean thoughts, impure desires, hateful attitudes. Everyone fits in there somewhere. And all need to be cleansed.

There can be no healing, cleansing, or forgiveness without a cleansing agent. And only the deep and eternal cleansing power from and by My Blood will bring restoration.

There can be nothing hidden, or it will never be removed.

So confess your sins daily—for all fail in one way or another. Be sure to 'do your wash' daily. That way, there will be no debris left to leave stains.

I died to cleanse and make you whole. I want to fill you and every place within you with My Presence. Make room for Me—confess the wrong, and I will replace it with My healing, forgiveness, and the balm of My love.

Once you have confessed these wrongs, let them go. Do not let the devil use them as tools against you. For I have cast them into the sea—I do not remember them and nor should you.

Let your hearts be filled with joy and rest in My Presence, for you belong to Me."

THE CHIPMUNKS

IN MY THOUGHTS, I saw two chipmunks, cute as could be, chattering together as if in conversation…then…

"Beware of chipmunks—so charming and so cute, yet so damaging. They collect their food and burrow deep down under the foundations of buildings. This can cause terrible risk to the strength and stability of the buildings.

Consider this: it is a clear picture of what gossip and criticism can do. You are a watchman. Be aware—if gossip starts, put an end to it. Do not participate in it. My body suffers greatly from this plague. Be a builder not a destroyer. You can find some good in everyone. If there is a difference of opinion, don't allow it to become destructive, or it will burrow a hole in the foundation of My temple. For it is founded on Me, not on opinion.

Guard against this even in your thinking—for it will damage your faith as well as others. You will find that your secret thoughts will come out by surprise one day and do damage you never intended to do.

Discussion is healthy and necessary, but when it becomes an argument, it will only turn into something whispered and personal.

This will weaken your spiritual health and foundation, and in that, it will weaken the strength of My body.

Every time you open your mouth, let it be a witness to My goodness, kindness, and understanding. Your mouth can be a door to My temple."

SERVING 'IN' WHO YOU ARE

LORD, HOW DO I serve You?

"By being fully you. Use all that you are are and wrap it in love, kindness, and wisdom.

What good is a bell that stands still. Its charm and purpose are only appreciated when it rings. Especially when it rings in rhythm.

It is the same with you. Moving in rhythm requires that you do what comes naturally—expressing your being by simply using your gifts, abilities, and heart with the natural sway that flows from who and Whose you are.

Don't try to be someone else—they have different gears and sounds. If you only knew the joy I get from watching the symphony of My body as it obeys and plays the instrument of 'uniqueness' in harmony with others who do the same.

Just as creation and seasons reveal their own magnificence and bring Me glory, so My body has its sounds and seasons of revelation that are meant to reveal Who I am in you. Just be all of who you are, and the fulfillment of who you are will also fill My body."

SKINNY

"SKINNY. PEOPLE SEEM to aim more at losing weight than gaining it. It is the opposite in the Spirit. The more of My Word you gain, the more beauty begins to shine. And when the weight of My glory rests on you, those around you will notice and be touched without even realizing why. So be sure the touch you leave is loving and kind, and the Spirit will make it personal.

Let those you pass on your path experience Me even when they don't know it. As they go forward, they will begin to recognize My touch, if only by its familiarity. Soon they will be on their own search to find Me, the source of their mystery.

So, be confident in your walk. Let there be no wasted steps. Your walk, which may seem ordinary to the onlooker, can be the turning point toward a heavenly eternity for those you don't even know.

The secret? Let Me walk in you."

WHO IS GOD?

EVERY DAY WE hear from the Lord about His love for us. His words are endless and freely express His heart. We are so appreciative of every word. And we thank Him for the way He pours it out on us daily.

But now I want to speak TO Him. I know without a doubt, you will join me.

I started my prayer time reading Psalm 95:6 in the NLT, "Come, let us bow down and worship; let us kneel before the Lord our maker."

I love this, but suddenly it seemed just so empty—so vague and distant. I realized how often we worship God, and rightfully so, for WHAT He is—God, Creator, King, and Lord.

But today I want to worship Him for WHO He is.

I thank Him for His kindness, His empathy, understanding, goodness, help, protection, nearness, our families, jobs, health, friends, our breath, the Holy Spirit, all of the intimate little moments when we know He is there, our homes, the love of our animals, safety, memories, His presence, our vacations, forgiveness, abilities, green grass, beautiful flowers, trees, cars, rain, food, sun, pools, favor, for making us Priests and Ministers to Him, for being our Father, His thoughtfulness, for speaking to us, for giving us warnings, for subduing our enemies, great food, for teaching us, for directing us, His righteousness, our descendants, for taking our punishment, for dying for us and rising and raising us to new life, for cleansing us and giving us a new heart, for making us His witnesses, for faith and knowing Him…and all those things we haven't even noticed yet.

His love acts in our lives before we ask, seek, or expect it. When we worship Him for these things, our hearts are touched and we enter into His heart which has depths we will never reach.

We may know Him for His glorious existence, but knowing Who He is, in us and for us, brings us to a whole new place.

I want to know more of Who He is.

YOU ARE A MIGHTY WEAPON

"WHEN YOU THINK you are alone, when you are in a battle and feel overpowered—look to the heavens and know that your help is there. I'll come in a power beyond yourself to help you fulfill your destiny, 'to become your future.'

I have destined you for greatness, for you will rule on the earth. You have a destiny far beyond what you can imagine. Here, it is to you, almost like a children's storybook—fun and exciting fantasy.

But your eternal purpose is far more than you can imagine. For now, just know that I am with you and that all you go through will be used to build you into a mighty servant. in your service to Me.

Fear not, for what seems unreal and beyond comprehension will become as natural as the heavenly breeze that will surround you. Trust Me. I know you don't understand. But, trust Me to do the work. You are only in the womb of your birth into eternal purpose."

THE ABUNDANT LIFE

"MY CHILD I have come that you might have life and have it abundantly.'" (John 10:10 ESV) How often must I say that word? Abundantly. This life I give you is in your heart and your spirit. It is the life of My Kingdom. All that is in Me is there. You satisfy yourself too easily, with two little. True joy is expressed by those who have an abundance of life within them.

How do you get this? Simple. Believe. Believe My promises as revealed in My Word. Don't pick and choose what you think might pertain to you. Learn to receive.

Have you ever seen a child standing there, watching you eat a piece of candy or something that they really wanted? They are so ready to receive from you and fully expect you to share what you have.

You are My children—I stand ready to hear your prayers. I know the 'panting' in your heart for Me to hear you. But I already have, and you have only to take and receive—but you can only receive by believing. And by believing, give testimony to the world."

FOLLOW MY PROMPTINGS

"DO NOT LIMIT My Presence to those times of worship, Scripture reading, or contemplation. I am always with you—I walk, pray, think, and move in you.

Your desires are not your own, but the response of the flesh is. Learn to follow your heart and let the flesh die.

Learn to recognize both My voice and My Hand in the promptings of your heart, and you will not only gain greater understanding but your own heart will be enlarged.

Learn to listen to the love expressed in your heart, not the limitations of your mind.

Learn to listen for peace and ignore the rattled, ungrateful, and unforgiving voice that rises from your depth.

Just as Elijah purified the water by throwing salt into its source, so you can change that murky depth by pouring My Word into the bottom of its well. There, it will become living water.

One step out of peace is one step into conflict.

Live in My Word and you will have peace."

LIVE IN TRUST

"WHEN YOU PRAY and you are worried about your problems—whether real or imagined—do you ever stop to think that the One to Whom you pray is the Almighty? Do you contemplate My power? Do you remember the Cross, the Ressurrection and the lengths I went to in order to save you and bring you out of that place you were so stuck in?

Learn to live in trust. It is a place, a home, where you can rest. Trust. Make it your new address. If you understood the joy I have when you do trust Me, you would find your own joy too.

There is no end to My power—I can do all things. I see you. I hear you. I love you. Will I not answer when you call? Look deep into your heart for that answer."

JUST BE MY VESSEL

"THE MORE YOU recognize your weakness, the more you will recognize My strength. See this as you do what you thought you were unable to do, for My strength is made perfect in your weakness. As you step out in faith, you make room for Me to move.

When you move in your own strength, you limit My Spirit by operating in your own fleshly will. Surrender to Me. Surrender your feelings of inadequacy and fear. Trust Me to move, speak and show My power. Don't restrict Me by your own confidence and boldness. Retreat, let your will and willingness subside, and give Me a place to release My glory and accomplish what you cannot do.

Always remember, I am the Savior. You are the vessel. When you understand that, you will never fear or feel unequipped, and you will be more and more encouraged to let Me use your presence to bring Mine."

IT'S NOT YOUR HEAD

I SAW A statue with the head being knocked off. At first I thought the Lord was going to speak about worshiping idols—but then—

"Get rid of your head. I didn't come to give life to your head or even to your thoughts—I came to give life to your spirit.

Life must be born in the spirit—and it follows that the mind will then be brought into conformity with and to My Spirit.

'Be sure you take time with Me. Come into the Holy of Holies.'

Worship and then come fully repentant, into My Presence, and be still. Do not speak. Take time to hear—but listen with your heart and receive the experience of My glory that will change you.

You will find an understanding that your mind cannot put into words. It is beyond you and beyond your heart to fully behold.

Yet, it will pour into you like warmth from a fire. The peace will almost be tangible, and it will heal all of the perplexities of your mind.

Nothing will need to make sense. You will simply know.

Like a mother cradling her baby, no words are needed or understood but enraptured by her love, the baby is at peace."

STOP RAISING WHAT'S DEAD

"DO YOU REALIZE that all of your struggles are between your mind and your spirit? It is an amazing thing to see.

Why do you waste so much of your energy when you could be putting it into confessing faith instead of going over and over the failures you have already confessed?

Don't continue to dwell on past mistakes. The moment they are confessed, they are gone. Why do you try so hard to bring them back?

Repeat My promises instead. Choose a promise relative to your need and then, like hammering a nail into a piece of wood, hammer it into your confusion, self-talk and unbelief.

You could start by remembering why I died. Then rejoice in My resurrection, and in that, your failures, sin and remorse are gone.

Love your new life. Your old life is dead, but your mind and your mouth are working very hard to raise it up."

THE PUZZLED PIECE

"PUZZLE PIECES—ALL THROWN together in a box, just waiting for you to put them together to make a picture. You try some, move some and press some into place.

This is a picture of My Body. All are moving around, trying to fit into places where they don't fit. Then when they find where they belong they find rest and peace. Only with everyone being in the right place will the full picture be seen.

The gifts and abilities I have given you are the expressed part of the picture that will complete the whole. I say expressed because this is a living picture—it is alive with My breath and touch. That is why you are so at peace and fulfilled when you are in the right place—because My full expression in you and through you brings others life and in turn, to you.

The picture in action—you see prophecy, healing, praying, writing, singing, composing, giving, nurturing, loving, comforting, feeding, helping, building, teaching, training...

What you don't see are all of the hidden hearts that are holding all of this together by their prayers and spiritual power. Seek the maturity of My Body operating in all of its capabilities. See the whole body functioning, and My life bringing blessings to all in need. Every activity brings Me glory and causes My body to grow.

I've already answered your prayerful questions, 'Where do I fit? What do I do?' The answers? Look within. Just look for what brings you life, and then that life will flow out to others. That life will give you energy and joy. You will both want and love to do what I have made you to do. Nothing else will satisfy you. Don't try to be like others. Can you imagine a puzzle with all the same pictures on each piece? Be free. Be you. Let your dreams, desires and abilities pour out of you and be used for the blessings of My Kingdom."

FAITHFULNESS

"WHAT DOES FAITHFULNESS really mean? Does it mean to have faith? To believe in Me and be filled with My Word? Or does it mean to belong, to be committed? Or maybe it means to not turn away from something or someone—to not give up?

It means all of these things.

1. FAITH: trusting Me.
2. BELONGING: you are Mine and I am yours.
3. BELIEVING: in Me and My Word
4. COMMITTING: yourself to Me as I have to you.

Why are you called 'the faithful'? Because you are all of these things. You are no longer defined or ruled by the world. You belong to Me and My Kingdom. Your heart is filled with the knowledge of Me, but your mind still wants to lead. Bring it into submission to your spirit. Always make your mind bow to the leading of My Spirit. This is how you achieve faithfulness.

"'You are My witnesses,' declares the Lord, 'and My servants whom I have chosen, so that you may know and believe Me and understand that I am HE. Before Me no God was formed, nor will there be one after Me. I, even I, am the Lord, apart from Me there is no other savior. I have revealed and saved and proclaimed—I, and not some foreign God among you. You are My witnesses,' declares the Lord, that I am God.'" (Isaiah 43:10-12 NIV)

It is for this reason that I called you, and it is for this reason that you must be filled with faith and therefore with faithfulness."

WHAT TIME IS IT?

A CLOCK. 11:10 -12:10. I'm not sure.

"Can you tell time? Are you aware of the eternal clock? Many seem to think that they have found or discovered the time of My return. Don't listen to them. It is not for them to know. Even the Son of Man does not know.

The important thing is not knowing when, but being ready. Spend less time searching and struggling as if you were going to find the answer and more time seeking the depths of the relationship you can have with Me while you are waiting. That's all that matters because no matter what, I will come for you in your lifetime.

Don't be like teenagers who have to run around, try everything, and pay no attention to their parents.

You will discover far more about this world by spending time with Me, for this is My world.

I want to reveal and share My secrets with you—to share all that I am and all that I originally planned for you in My world.

I have removed sin, and now I want to restore you to your original glory, even despite the corruption that still remains in creation. You don't have to be a part of that corruption, for in you is life, truth, and spirit. You can be all you see—as you dwell in Me.

I want to be the One that feeds you, loves you, teaches you, and leads you."

STEP BY STEP

"YOUR EARNESTNESS IS growing, and soon it will break through a wall and bring you to a higher place of faith.

Consider your schools. You learn step by step as each grade leads you higher and you develop more understanding, comprehension, and liberty. Finally, you are on your own—and ready to function in the place and ministry of your calling. That function is like a graduate school as you apply all you have learned to actual circumstances. You will not be an expert the day you enter but will continue to learn by your daily experience.

Your spiritual education will never end, but you must learn 'as you go,' so to speak. When you were born again, you began to see with new eyes and have a hunger for more of what you have never known.

When discouragement hits, know use it to push you forward—to help you continue choosing Me, whether you understand or not. It is the choice to move forward, understanding will come later. But when you find that understanding, you will realize that you are on a new level and ready to move into a new depth.

That new depth is in your intimacy with Me and the knowledge that secures your heart and breaks off any unbelief.

You don't know or understand your walk, but I have guided and will guide every step. Walk in My light and have no fear. Fear is just a stop sign put there by the devil to stop you from moving forward. Take your hammer and destroy it with My Word."

MY GRIEF

"THE DEEP GRIEF you feel is the fall of sin and the actual effects of it.

Death, sin, separation. You accept My saving work but without experiencing the emotional pain that brought Me there.

The pain you feel is the very pain that brought Me to the cross and the pain I felt from that very first fall.

Separation, rejection, hurt, lack of trust, death in the garden—death to a glorious life that only knew happiness and blessings.

The pain that brought Me to the cross was worse than the pain of the cross. Creation's reaction to the victory I won there was only a spark compared to what happened in heaven.

So, when you grieve, stop to contemplate the grief I had losing you to sin and the thunderous reaction of creation to your restoration.

I love you. Plain and simple. Nothing to figure out or explain. I just love you and celebrate the grief that empowered My saving work."

EMPOWERED READING

"THE POWER OF My Word. It can invade your heart. It can enlighten your mind. Or it can stay on the page and be read as any other book.

The choice is always yours. If you read it with your mind, you can meditate on it, memorize it, and I can speak to you in a personal way.

If you read it with a heart that has just been filled with worship, it will all become life to you. Even without a personal message, even if you don't understand it, you will feel life invading you, sometimes bringing you to the point of tears.

For My Word is life. It gives life and healing to the body. It carries life beyond your understanding, filling the cells of your being and causing an excitement of hunger to rise within you for all that it contains.

So don't just read the word. Worship Me in it and through it, and you'll find ever-increasing life that will never leave."

THE VISION OF MY HEART

"MY CREATION IS a picture of My heart. When I created the world, I created it in and for peace and love. I filled it with good things that would express that love—good food, good health, and experiences that would help you know and experience My touch and Who I am.

Clear water to wash, soak, swim in, and refresh you.

Sun to keep you warm and smile on you. Shade to give you relief and rest. Rock hard things to give you support when needed and to use when building places of protection. Soft things—animals to touch, love and bring My tenderness. Even toddlers and babies love soft stuffed animals. They all serve a purpose. The need to touch and be touched—to hold something close and hug. This is so important and can come from many directions.

All are extensions of My Hand—to hold, love, and experience the miracle and healing warmth reaching into your hearts. That's why the laying on of hands is so important. It again is the miracle of touch that warms the whole heart and soul. Even on strangers, the touch of one or many hands brings instant acceptance and care for whatever their needs are.

The kiss from a dog or the purr of a kitten bring joy and healing to lonely hearts of the elderly.

I made it all—yield to Me. Rest and soak in these truths and you'll find My touch every day."

YOU ARE MY ROSE

"ROSES—SOME WITH BLEMISHED petals, some with fallen petals, and some in full bloom.

You are all at different stages of beauty, but all are roses nonetheless.

Blossoms need lots of sun—without it they will not come into full bloom. They need lots of water to keep their roots and soil moist.

You are My rose. The more time you spend with the SON, the more perfectly you will bloom.

The water of revelation will cause you to bear more blossoms, and its life will bring a fragrance to every rose in My garden.

Imagine a vase. In it is a bouquet filled with My children—with no imperfect blossoms and a fragrance that cannot be imagined—as I present it holy and blameless to My Father. Oh, the joy in My heart as I look to that day.

You are My rose. Let Me fill you with My light and My Word. Take time to draw in these sources of growth so that you will blend in beautifully, in full bloom.

Take this to heart. Don't think it will happen naturally. Just as your body needs food and water, so does My Garden. Make My joy complete by blossoming in My care."

A RAGGED SOUL

"A RAGGED SOUL. It looks good on the outside, but it has no life or strength. Do you? Are you eating the right food? Are you chewing it and digesting what you eat? Do you eat everything on your plate at the same time, or do you take one bite at a time and slowly chew it and send it into your system? Or do you scoop it all up, mixing the food, not enjoying or tasting each food individually?

So it is with your spiritual food. When you read the Word, you are putting food on your plate. Take time to let Me feed you, one teaspoon at a time—don't read and run. Take it slowly, chew it slowly, swallow the meaning, and let it become a part of you. Let it enter your heart and it will slowly enter your mind, expanding its understanding. It is not how much you eat but what you eat and how often you take the time to assimilate it. This is what you feed your spiritual man and what gives him muscle.

My desire is not just to serve a banquet but to let each dish be a banquet on its own. Go over some of the things I have shown you. Make a list. Then taste it all again, one food at a time. Tighten the ropes, so to speak.

Do this and that limp doll will become much stronger than you thought, ready to walk in power and destroy the enemy. Only believe."

BE GUIDED BY MY WORD

"TRUTH IS REALITY. Anything else is a distortion from man.

No one believed the earth was round. Did that change its shape? Neither will one man's opinion change the shape of My Word.

Man makes it so complicated. When you are confused, just come to Me.

If a door is open, who opened it? If a door is closed, who closed it? No one but Me. My Word opens the door both to faith and to understanding. When you try to find your answers in man, you will only get man's mind. Carry My Word in your heart and you will move in power. You can overcome centuries of unbelief and distorted ideas by just believing My Word.

Look to your weakness. Do you see where you are lacking? Find My promise concerning your weakness and receive it into your inner being.

This is not to say that you shouldn't enjoy good counsel. But if the counsel doesn't line up with My Word, don't accept it.

Weakness, unbelief, confusion, and fear all try to make you conform to the human mind.

Let My Spirit 'rain' on you. Sit before Me and enjoy the 'shower.' Let Me cleanse you from the ashes of men and build in you the Rock of Ages."

THE LIVING WATERS

"I SAW A pool of water with a continual flow of water coming from a raised spout above it and pouring into the pool.

It was all living water—clear and beautiful. The pool was being filled but was also pouring its water out over the edge into all of the world, and I heard…

"It is there for all, but not all will drink from it. They prefer their own 'cisterns' that hold polluted water—polluted by their own making and thinking. This water is murky—not clear and refreshing. It's just enough to satisfy the very small thirst of man.

It takes so little to satisfy them—they fill their minds instead of their hearts. And they go on refilling themselves with the same cloudy ideas that satisfy the limits of their thinking.

This is why you must fill your hearts with My living water daily. You must be ready to pour that water out wherever you go. There, leave refreshment, leave healing, hope and grace. Be the spout that leaves the pool of living water that comes from within you—and pour out all I have given you. Create hunger by who you are. Give the drink that never stops but at the same time, yearns for more. Wash hurt and heal wrong thinking by bringing the light of truth. Raise closed eyes to Me and cause them to open their hearts.

Every day begin your day by surrendering to Me. Then, I am free to cause the 'flowers' in the garden of your life to begin to bloom."

THE FERRIS WHEEL

I SAW A Ferris wheel. It had lots of little lights, but my attention was drawn more to the inner part—the motor that energized the motion of the wheel. It too, was going in a circular motion, and its motion was causing the larger wheel to go around. I thought, "Oh Lord—I don't have a clue about a Ferris wheel…"

He said,

"The inner workings are a picture of your mind, and it shows how effortlessly it encircles your thoughts and actions, continually giving directions to your thoughts—the same thoughts over and over again, ultimately resulting in the same actions. 'Round and round' you go, doing the same things over and over. The same thoughts and the same response.

Turning it off is really very easy—just turn the switch. The hard part is recognizing what's happening and being willing to shut it down.

Those thoughts, worries and mental activities can rob you, discourage you and cause fear and hopelessness. They can run and ruin your life.

Turn to Me—and I will turn off the switch. I will give you new thoughts, new visions, new hope, and the power to move out of the circle and into a new direction.

Get off the wheel and follow Me—the light is much brighter where I am, the thoughts will lead you where you haven't been, and the result will be having My mind and not your own."

THE NOTEBOOK

I WAS SITTING before the Lord with my notebook and pen waiting to hear from Him.

My eyes were drawn to the three holes on the edge of my spiral notebook. I pictured them going into a three ring binder but only attached by two holes and realized how that would just cause the paper to tear and not be in "union" with the purpose of the paper.

I heard:

"So it is with your relationship with the Trinity. I am your SAVIOR—I paid the price for your sin with the suffering and shedding of My Blood. It is My Blood that cleanses you. I died and rose from the dead and returned to the FATHER. He loves you and sent Me to make your way back to Him by removing the sin that separates us. I left My Word with you and sent you My HOLY SPIRIT to reveal the Father's love and give you insight and understanding into the depths of that love found in My Word. He will remain with you and give you wisdom and understanding along with the power to do the work of sharing My love with others.

Father, Son, and Holy Spirit all holding you together in each page of your life. It is the work of your God moving in all aspects of your days to keep you secure in faith. We together are one God, operating in three different ways. You will never understand this, but you will experience it if you keep your heart open and receive the fullness of Who I am."

WHAT ARE THOSE DOTS?

I SAW A paper filled with dark blue dots, countless in number. I kept trying to set it aside, thinking this couldn't be the Lord. What am I to do with these dots??? And then I heard…

"Can you see what I see? No, you just see the dots on a page… and they leave you with questions and confusion. You tend to disregard them because they make no sense to you. You don't see what I see, and so, you put it aside and ignore what is in front of you.

But what don't you see? You don't see what I am forming, you don't see the finished work.

The dots are symbolic of your life. Things you have experienced, loved, accomplished, or wished for. They are all separate, seemingly unattached and unrelated to anything you can understand.

Can you imagine what you would think or do with all of creation and its contents before I spoke it out? Yet look—look at the beauty and the riches of the universe. Would you have ever been able to imagine that?

So, treasure those 'dots,' for they are the components of your eternal destiny. You just have to walk and keep your eyes on Me, and I will bring to your life an eternal form and beauty with a purpose you cannot imagine.

Trust Me, for I will bring it all together and your life will shine and sparkle like the universe.

Just dots on the page? No, they form a living, eternal promise."

AN IMPERFECT FLOWER

"A FLOWER—ONE PETAL is broken. Is it still a flower? Of course.

Once you are born again, you cannot be unborn. You may not come into full bloom, or you may drop a petal, but you are still a flower. And once placed in a bouquet, no one would even notice it. It is covered, so to speak.

So learn to cover your brother's nakedness. Work to reveal each other's beauty. In your private relationship, you must speak the truth in love, but only in private and not until you have a deep understanding about what you speak. You can make the broken petal bloom again by your kindness—understanding is the balm of My Spirit. Harshness destroys and causes My 'flowers' to wilt—and remember, it is yours to nurture, not to hurt.

Don't take on problems that are beyond you—you do not have all the answers—but lead always with love. That is always your part.

Honor each other. Wash each other's feet by submitting to My ministry to you, and through you. You will get more pleasure and joy out of being used by Me than you will out of working your own plan.

I am the gardener—let Me use you to nurture My garden. I will do the weeding when it's time—you have only to water it with the goodness of My Spirit."

THE LIGHT OF MY PRESENCE

"FIREPLACE, FIRECRACKERS, FIREWORKS. Which would you prefer?

A warm fire burns in its place and is peaceful and comforting. You can rest by it and even sleep there amid its dimly lit light and rest in My Presence.

Or you may be alert to the firecrackers—they are quick to snap and burn with flashes of light that come and go, yet fill you with excitement. Those are the small, quick insights and revelations of My Holy Spirit that you receive as you go through your day.

Fireworks!!! Large splashes of power and thunderous sound, clearly seen by all. Those who watch are filled with an experience of power they don't understand. It is the place of miracles! The things that outshine them all! Places filled with the power and activity of My Spirit.

Which one do you choose? I have Good News!! You don't have to make a choice!

There is a time and a place for each of these lights. It is so often thought that one is wrong and another is right. Why do My people limit Me? They try to fit Me into such a limited space. Do you think I am limited?

Look to the universe. Do you see an end or a beginning? There is always light somewhere, and there is always a time of rest somewhere else. But it is all of Me.

I give you what you ask for. Seek and you shall find. Just learn to live in My presence. Get excited at the daily revelations of Who I am and expect the thunder of My voice and the wondrous light of My miracles."

MY THOUGHTS

"MY HEART HEARS your heart. I know your thoughts, ways, and struggles. Those are what I saved you from. You know you are saved, yet you continue to try to save yourself. Learn to carry My Presence. Be aware of it and simply let it move your actions and your words. I promise you—I will do a better job!

Yield to Me—My way is always love. Love never loses. It never ignites anger—it always prepares the way for peace.

Is there an unresolved issue that you struggle with? Add love. Is there a difficult person? Add love. Is there a painful memory? Conquer it with an equally strong loving memory.

Always look for the good. When something or someone irritates you, look—sincerely look—for the good.

Be careful of the thoughts that you entertain. Hurtful, painful thoughts only bring more pain. Concentrate on the good and you'll see its revelation grow before your eyes.

Most importantly—pray and bless the person or circumstance with whatever is required. You will see the victory arise like the sun."

THE DEAD PALM BRANCH

I SAW A dead palm frond hanging from its tree...

"There is always a process at work. New growth comes in, the old dies out. In the world, this seems sad, but in My world it is a picture of victory. Life always wins out. The branch you saw this morning is a beautiful picture—My Body died only that it might live forever. And, as you exhibit your spiritual growth by letting the old stuff die, new growth will appear. Old habits, emotions, activities, attitudes, sinful thoughts, deeds—you will see new life take their place. New attitudes and actions will become natural and even more common than the old ones. I rejoice in this as I do in the forming of a newborn child.

It is a new life. It has a new purpose and ability. It is filled with love and forgiveness. The old has died—but the new lives forever."

THE SILENT BELL

THIS MORNING AFTER my prayer time, I saw a lot of small bells in different colors. I asked the Lord what they meant. I was led to look it up and saw that bells are holy to the Lord, like the bells on the bottom of the High Priest's garment.

There are many meanings, but all are attached to a form of celebration—like bells at Christmas, Easter, graduation, blessings, beginnings, and endings. Wedding bells, worship bells—they are always signs of celebration or accomplishment. A time of moving onto the next thing or grade or promotion—of going onward and upward!

Bells are a sound of joy and love. Picture the romantic movies. They always end with a soft snowfall, a silent moment as they look up, and then—the bells start ringing and everybody stands smiling, in awe. With that, the story ends.

I wondered why the Lord put this on my heart so strongly, and I felt like He was saying to pay attention to the bells in our lives. Those times that are kind of a right of passage—a sign of deeper revelation, the courage to do a new thing, the forgiveness of a long-held grudge, or someone's accomplishment.

My first response was to want to run out and buy a little bell that I could ring at a time of celebration, even over little tiny things. In other words, to live our lives in a spirit of celebration, living in gracious gratitude for the blessings He gives.

Then, I remembered that I already have a bell—high above the bookcase in the den where I can't reach. And it hasn't been rung in years.

I have to wonder—why does anybody have a bell and never ring it?

DON'T BE AFRAID

OH LORD, YOU are a shield about me, my glory and the lifter of my head…
Psalm 3:3b ESV)

"Your sorrows are My sorrows. I live in you and experience all you feel.

My understanding brings you peace, and it resolves the issues the devil uses to accuse you every day.

You pray to stand on My side and be the deciding witness of My truth. You can easily do that by just standing in My love and My promises—then you'll be standing on My side automatically.

No need for formulas—just do, say, and stand in what is right and you will be standing with Me.

Always look up—beyond yourself—and trust Me. As you look into the universe and see My greatness, let its reality strengthen your faith.

Don't be afraid, for I am with you. Don't be discouraged, for I am your God. I will strengthen you and help you. I will hold you up with my victorious right hand.

'(Isaiah 41:10 NLT)'"

BREAK THE BLOCKS

"THERE ARE BLOCKS that come into your mind—thoughts to keep your attention from Me. They work to cause confusion and distraction.

The devil uses them and erects them to draw your attention and cause chatter! Chatter that prevents you from entering My peaceful presence.

When you hear this chatter, realize that these are not your thoughts, they are created to interrupt you and make it very difficult for you to focus.

See it as an annoying parrot that repeats the same thing over and over. Just command it to leave. Learn to let your heart lead and make a deliberate choice to avoid the devil's tactics. Sing praises, worship, and keep praying. He won't be able to stay—he will run.

Don't let him make your mind his playground. Let your mind be a place he hates to go."

THE LILIES

I SAW BEAUTIFUL white lilies on the ceiling of the Holy of Holies. The ceiling was filled with them. I stopped to look up the meaning for lilies. They are a symbol of purity, fertility, innocent beauty, fresh life, and rebirth. I asked the Lord what it all meant...

"Every day, spend time worshiping and coming into My Presence. You will experience this fresh life and rebirth over and over again. In Me there is no time, so each time can be the first time, yet each time builds on the time before.

You have the freshness of the beginning and the experience of your growth—both at the same time. That is because you are always beginning. There is no end. You always have just as far to go. If you live in My Presence, you will grow in knowledge of Me, yourself, your purpose, and the depth of love.

You will forgive each other as I have forgiven you. You will always leave a blessing and a touch of love. The Mercy Seat in the Holy of Holies is not just for you but also for you to bring to others. So have mercy.

'Consider the lilies—they neither toil nor spin.' (Matt. 6:28 ESV) Be at peace and carry their innocent beauty—enjoy the freedom of new life every day.

Rest in the Holy of Holies, and your transformation will bloom like the lilies. You can fill each moment, thought and action while you carry the very presence of God. You are My lilies in the field."

FALSE HOPE

"PEOPLE NEED HOPE. They find and believe in the craziest things, 'hoping' it will bring good luck or a change of events.

Isn't it odd—they can believe and actually trust in a four leaf clover, a rabbit's foot on a chain, or all kinds of magic, as if any of these things hold an answer to their dreams or needs. Yet they cannot believe in or turn to Me, their maker.

In Me is their lifeblood and eternity, yet they will trust in the leaf of a plant or a toy so easily. It truly shows the limitations of the human mind.

That is why I ask for your heart. The heart will not accept these small, man-made ideas—only the mind, which is so limited by its own perceptions, will give place to these counterfeits.

The heart? That is made for Me. If it remains empty of My Presence, I cannot bring it to the eternal place prepared for it. But, if it yearns for My Presence, if it lets Me fill it by giving it over to My love, it's whole life, purpose, and fulfillment are changed forever.

Such a simple thing. Try it. Cast away your hope in lifeless things, put it in Me, and come to life. Things will fade, break and be tossed away. But a heart alive in Me will find joy, life and fullness that will continue to grow for all eternity."

THE LORD'S PRAYER

THIS CAME AS I was praying the Lord's prayer this morning.

My Father...

I am born in you. You love and care for me as no one else can or will.

Who art in Heaven...

The place where You wait for me and where I will be safe in Your arms.

Hallowed be Thy Name...

Oh, the unsurpassed joy at the glory of Your Name being exalted above all the earth and throughout the universe.

Thy Kingdom come...

Let this glory come to the earth filled with the unending light of Your honor and holiness.

Thy will be done on earth as it is in Heaven...

Embedded in us by Your habitation.

Give us this day our daily bread...

Jesus, You are the bread of life. Feed us continually with revelation, wisdom, and the love of the Father.

And lead us not into temptation...

To not walk alone but only with You that we may carry Your Presence continually.

And forgive us our trespasses as we forgive those who trespass against us...

Give us such understanding as we see ourselves in others, and therefore, forgiving what we see because we see ourselves.

But deliver us from evil...

From falling backward into our weaknesses and doing the will of the devil instead of yours.

For Thine is the Kingdom, the power, and the glory forever and ever...

In heaven, on earth, and in us, Amen.

THE WAY OF PEACE

IN PRAYING FOR the world, this is what I heard…

"My heart aches for those who love Me. And even more for those who don't.

Do not parents rejoice in seeing the child they love doing the right thing and making the right choices? Aren't they filled with love and warm hearts?

But, what about the child who makes wrong decisions? Do they love this child less? No, behavior doesn't change love, it just changes the response. But instead of a warm heart, the parents have a painful heart that drives love even deeper. They are filled with exasperation, along with a desperate love that seeks healing and restoration for that child.

So it is with My Father—He loves all of His children. But they all became the child that brought Him to the desperation of the cross, through Me.

So how then, can anyone sink so deep into their unworthiness, that they can't experience My love? What a tremendous deception of the devil!

It is exactly that unworthiness that caused Me to lay down My life. All are unworthy—all have sinned and been redeemed. Don't let guilt, shame, or the devil's ugly lies keep you from Me. The price has been paid for your sin—you have only to receive it and be forgiven.

Even after experiencing the cross, there are those who hide or deny themselves the experience of My life.

If you have confessed your sins and received My forgiveness, you are free and able to forgive others. So let's start with you—forgive yourself. Then your heart will be open to walk with and forgive others."

THE TRUE ACT OF FAITH

"THE HEART OF the Father waits for you. He longs to hold you and all your cares in His arms. He has such joy in your coming and making yourself ready through the surrender of all you hold dear.

Do you trust Him? Or, are you hesitant? Do you think the reward for seeking Him is bittersweet? Or do you trust His love enough to trust Him with all you hold in your heart? Your goal should be to lay against his breast without worry or concern, knowing you can trust Him with it all.

Man seems to pray with one hand and hold onto everything in his life with the other. Let it go. Enjoy His joy. Worry is a thief that both robs you and deposits in you its own fear.

His arms are the place of perfect trust that bring true peace and certain victory. What loving father draws you close only to discard your cares and needs? Do you want more victory in your life? Do you yearn to be closer to your Father? The quick path, with no waiting, is trust.

You will find that trust in rest is the true act of faith."

JUST ASK ME

"I AM ALWAYS here, waiting for you. Go ahead, ask Me questions. I love speaking with you—sharing your tears and healing your hurts. I want to bring you faith and understanding.

Some people read books, ask friends, listen to sermons—all of these things are good—but they don't come to Me personally and simply ask.

I am always here for you. Don't take the long trip through a maze—just come straight to Me. Then, I can lead you to answers, and you won't have to question whether it is THE answer.

When you seek wisdom, you will find it. When you seek answers, you will find comfort as well. I want you to be at peace—so come, reach out, and you will receive what you need.

I see you. I know the hurt—it is not from Me, but I will heal it. Trust Me. As you rest against My breast, goodness and kindness will heal your heart, and a relationship you never expected will be born or increase. There is no end to My depths, so all things are always new."

CAN I USE YOUR HAND?

"BE STILL AND watch. Make a habit of looking for My Hand. Pray to be aware of My Presence.

I am always with you—you never walk alone. If you do not know that, your eyes are not open. I speak of the eyes of your heart. They can see far more than your physical eyes. They see not only the outside, but they see the inside too.

Who are you with? Who are you talking to? Where do you have to go? Who will you meet there? You can make every moment a miracle. Maybe man will never see it, but you will, if you see it with your inner eyes. It will be at work, causing a change of heart or direction. It will cause a light, a smile, a thought, or an idea.

Is it a kind word? Is it an encouraging thought? A helping hand—like that of an angel? An understanding heart? A physical need? My hand is always reaching out. Can I use yours?

Open the eyes of your heart. Let the light shine out and let My Presence be seen.

In turn, the light in you will grow brighter and greater. And I will cherish our working together."

HE'S JUST ALWAYS THERE

I HAD HAD a busy day and not had my usual morning time with the Lord. I was really tired, and I settled into what I thought would be a short prayer time… and it was… but He did all the talking.

"There are times to be at rest—that is important. Your body needs rest and sleep. So does your mind. However, your spirit is your watchman. It never rests…it is eternal. Your body is a wall between you and heaven. It limits you. But your spirit is the doorway to My presence and to the heavenlies. That is why it is so much better to seek Me in the early hours. When you are rested, the trinity of your body, soul, and spirit are in accord.

So meet Me early and be filled in the fullness of your being. I am always there for you—I don't sleep, I wait—just for you."

His kindness overwhelms me.

MELT THE BUTTER

"ALL CREATION BOWS to Me. Yet man refuses to bow.

Who is man that he should do this? Does he think he rules that which gave him birth? Imagine that!

So for My sake, be careful as you minister as My vessel. Let your words, actions, and prayers be for those who are lost. If those words and actions come through a pure and loving vessel, they will not only be received in peace, but they will weaken the hardened heart. Remember, it is not you who saves—it is I. Don't just share words—take your time—share goodness, mercy, and kindness.

When you melt butter in a pan, do you do it on a high heat or on a slow-burning, low heat? You do it carefully, slowly stirring it. In the same way, melt the hearts of those you pray for carefully. Don't be in a rush to change their minds. Rather, through your quiet and consistent stirring, change their hearts—their minds will follow and gradually melt as well.

Then, that 'butter' will melt into My 'bread' and become one pure and holy loaf."

WHOSE YOU ARE

AS I STARTED my prayer time this morning with the Scripture, "How great are You Oh Sovereign Lord! There is no one like You and there is no God but You," (2Samuel 7:22 NIV) I had an experience I've never had before.

As I prayed, I was suddenly brought into an awareness of His Majesty as never before. Now, it was not as if I had an experience of going to heaven or anything like that; it was simply that I was very aware of Who He is. There I was, with His splendor, power and authority, yet no sense of His love, though love wasn't absent.

I can't find a word to explain or express this Majesty—it just made me unable to really speak or make sense, at least in the English language. So I was speechless. I tried asking forgiveness for taking Him for granted and everything I could think of, but compared to Him, it all sounded like nonsense. I realized that there was nothing I could say. My mouth was shut tight as if I couldn't speak.

I was just so aware of His mind, power and splendor that the idea of resting on His chest or any of those loving experiences we've had became so absolutely foreign that I could not find words, even for my thoughts.

I tried to recapture the feeling of His love. But His splendor just wouldn't let me go there. Again, it's not that I actually experienced this—it's hard to describe—I just became very acutely aware of these things. **Then as I sat there, I was led to look at His feet and there, in a very tiny, small form like a dot of black, was the devil.**

I realized, with joy, the power of God over him and the power He has given to us.

The awesome strength, power, and authority of God spoke so kindly as He said…

"Now do you understand your authority and WHOSE you are?"

LIFE HERE AND LIFE THERE

"TEARS, JOY, HIGHS, lows. It's all just a part of the life you live on earth. No one is happy or sad all of the time. There are trials, tribulations, and things that will rob you both of the joy of life and of life itself.

But I came to bring you life, eternal life—where there are no tears, no sickness or death but only joy, and it will last forever.

Oh the frustration and the pain of offering a gift of this magnitude and watching those who turn away and refuse it.

There will come a time when the door will be closed, the stairway will be pulled up, and all light will be removed. The sounds of joy will fill the heavens while others dwell in darkness and pain.

Pray hard and consistently for souls to be saved. Pray for a hunger in their hearts and the desire for truth to turn them to Me.

Pray that the gift of My life for them will be recognized and received.

Pray for harvesters—those who will seek out the lost and touch them with the power of love.

Pray for a great homecoming, a great celebration, and a great harvest.

I am 'not willing that any should perish, but that all should come to repentance.' (2 Peter 3:9 BLB) May all who hear the message of My love surrender to Me and live in joy eternally."

IT'S ALL ENDLESS

"THE WORLD IS beautiful to see. Indeed, it is amazing. But even more so, it all has a purpose and a parable of sorts. It tells a story. Never again will you look at it the same way—not once you start looking for its message, its story.

All of what I have made is not just to provide beauty and sources of life, look beyond that and find the meaning of its presence. It speaks of Me. The endless height and bottomless depth. The mountains speak of the presence of My power and always cry out, 'Come up higher.'

A calm river provides food, water, and continual cleansing. It speaks of the gentleness of My work within you and the refreshment it brings.

The ocean is endless as it moves, connects, and surrounds the world. There is a place and a sound for every land—yet its spirit speaks the same language.

Look at the endless shapes, colors, and sizes of beauty. The supply of this artistry never ends, there is always more to discover.

All of this, not to mention the inhabitants. The birds and animals, all with purpose and means of survival. You will never discover all there is. When you think you have seen it all, you have only just begun to see. The beginning of new discoveries and their meaning is endless.

And now, look at you. I have given you authority over all of these things, and yet you haven't even begun to discover yourself. There are within you heights and depths that you can't imagine and have never touched. As I have no beginning or end, so at the end of your life, you have only just begun.

Pray for eyes to see Me in everything you look at in My world, and you will find that you are enveloped by Me. As you are enveloped by Me, you will discover more of yourself."

HOME DELIVERY

"ON THE HORIZON, the sun is seen, rising in its glory! A new day! What will it bring? In the glory, comes power—power to bring answers to your prayers, power to heal and to save. The power is there, but where are the servants to administer My power? Where are those who will deliver it, speak it, release it, and empower others?

I have given you a vision of My authority—use it. Walk in it. Don't be timid, be earnest.

Hear My voice within you—listen for it—and don't be afraid or discouraged. What you see when you bring My Word or My love is only the external. But I will be working in their inner being.

When you deliver something or leave a package on the porch, you don't stay and see them open it. You only deliver it. That's all I ask. I will be the one to open the Word you speak or the gift you bring and use it to reveal My heart.

You see sheep leaving the fold and going alone, each in its own direction. These are not lost sheep, they are each responding to their call and will return.

Deliver, speak, give, do what I give you to do, and then come back. Obedience, no matter how small, will bear much fruit.

You carry within you My Kingdom. There is always a supply ready for you to share with those I put in your life. You don't have to do all the work from start to finish, you just have to give or plant what I put in your heart, your mouth, or your hand. Just be My faithful servants."

SPEAK TO THE ETERNAL

"WHAT TIME IS it? Do you know? I need you to live as if there is no time. Your flesh needs a schedule, but your spirit should always be with Me. Always be in the place of ministry, even if it is only to yourself.

Feed the power of My Spirit and His ministry into your well. Listen to Him speak. Keep your spiritual ears open.

Then follow His lead. Your time is His time. He will offer you both rest and ministry. Keep your eyes open. Who is in front of you? Prophecy is not always for meetings and church—it is for all the needs you might find in your day. My spirit has no time clock or physical place to minister. You are His place. My work is for My body to come alive. Speak out, reach out and touch those in your path—fill the atmosphere with My presence.

Can you imagine the difference it would make if all of My children did this? I have given you an open pathway and this path is in the Spirit. It is the open hearts that I reach for and am hungry for My children.

My work is eternal. So speak and minister to the eternal."

WE PRAY WHAT HE PRAYED

AS I TOOK the bread of communion today, I started to cry. I had been praying so hard for our country—against abortion, socialism, atheism, and all the anti-God movements. I was imploring God for His help when suddenly, as I took the bread and began to chew, I cried, realizing that all I was asking for was the very reason Jesus came. In other words, **He came to bring the answers to the prayers we haven't even prayed yet**. What I was asking for was the very thing that brought Him to the earth.

He laid down His life long ago to bring righteousness, forgiveness, restoration, healing, and faith. That's why our prayers have to start with thanksgiving.

We need to take a stand and do all we can for the sake of righteousness. He has called us to do the work of bringing His love to our world.

We are praying with His heart, His earnestness, His love, and His vision as His heart finds expression in our words.

All we are called to be is found in His Heart.

EASTER IN THE WINTER

"EASTER IS COMING! The power of the Resurrection!

Your country is dying—what you see and hear is the voice of death, and it's simply a result of the choices it has made.

But now, My power is moving to resurrect your world—to restore its health, its strength, and its power. How? By returning to Me, the giver of life.

You see an ant. It is followed by another and another and another, not scurrying but marching in a line that has a purpose, and seems to never end.

So it is with My people. They are coming one by one, following the lead—not sure of where they are going but sure of the direction they are moving in. This is My body—just keep in step with Me and you will find that you are accomplishing My work. For nothing I do is idle or temporary. It all works together to accomplish My will. So be faithful—do what the Spirit leads you to do, no matter how small, and when it all comes together, there will be a glorious restoration."

SOMETIMES IT'S TOO BRIGHT

"SOMETIMES, TOO MUCH light will blind you. Your eyes have to slowly adjust to the increasing light. You can see the light ahead and imagine its glory, but you miss all of the light and revelation lost in its brilliant beams.

That is why I give you small amounts of light—just a little at a time. Then, you won't miss anything. It is one thing to see a vision and yet another to understand it.

Focus on the daily words I give you, and as you grow closer to the glory, you will bring with you an understanding you otherwise would not have.

Just as particles enhance reality, so the lesser light will begin to enrapture your whole being. Then I can bring you into the fullness of that light and all it contains rather than just a vision of it.

You may have a 'brilliant' experience, but what will you get out of it? Just an experience. But if you move slowly, gradually increasing your light, you'll have a much greater understanding of what you are experiencing.

So don't think you are not growing through your daily commitment to Me—it is all adding up to a much greater revelation rather than a one-time experience.

I ask you, this question, 'Do you want to truly know Me or just observe or witness My presence from afar?'"

THE FRUIT OF YOUR WORK

"CARRYING MY CROSS doesn't mean literally—it means to carry out the purpose I have put in you. It will be a combination of hardship and joy. Commit to it and it will prove to be the deepest, most satisfying experience found in your reason for living.

The purpose I have given you will last for eternity, and you will see the fruit of your work forever. It will never fail or even wear out.

Accept this call, take hold of it, and see it done.

It may be loving people, helping people, writing, playing or singing music, working with children—whatever is in you. It wants to live.

Surrender to its life within you and bring it out—it is an eternal work.

The day will come when you will see the fruit of what you've done displayed in heaven."

THE HEALING OF THOUGHTS

"COME TO THE garden. Sit beside Me. Look into My eyes. Use your imagination. You will never be the same.

I know how you feel, but it would be good for you to express it. Then, as you identify your feelings, I will speak to you and bring understanding that leads to healing. It will deepen your awareness of My presence while bringing peace to your questiong heart. Sharing your hidden feelings will also free you from negative thoughts about yourself. I say, 'you are man—you are flesh.' The day will come when you will be free of flesh, and the holy new man that resides within you will be seen. Until then, help Me to help you by dealing with those thoughts. Imagine our conversation and you will come into forgiveness and love. So don't just pray words and confess sins, come to Me and discuss it. Enjoy the union with Me, and the oneness we share will overwhelm the flesh and the self-thoughts that work against you.

Simply put, come into true relationship with Me."

THE LIFE I HAVE
PREPARED FOR YOU

"DO YOU REALLY think your life ends here? Do you think the gifts, dreams, and abilities I have given you are only for this world?

The evil has been dethroned. The good, the extraordinary and the exceptional will live forever. The life you have here is only a taste of what you'll be doing in eternity. What you see and experience here is only a tug in the direction you are going.

This life you live is as darkness compared to what is ahead. In the new earth, you will experience the glory you have only imagined.

Do what you love to do and do it well. Don't be afraid to stretch yourself— you were made to stretch and reach unknown and unexpected places. Do your best and what you don't achieve here, you will achieve there.

Do you think that when you die you are at the end of life? Trust Me—you have only just begun."

WHEN DOES ETERNAL LIFE BEGIN

"SELF-HATE IS AS destructive as death. Self-love is equally destructive because it has no room for the life of others or for Me.

You can know how much My love lives and rules in you by how much you die to yourself. When you let your flesh die, you make room for more of My love to flow within you.

I laid down My life to give you life. Will you not lay down yours to let My life live in you?

The life that causes you to breathe, think, and act dies. The life that I give is eternal and will never die.

You can choose daily for the power of eternity to rule within you. You do not have to die to experience it—it was born in you the moment you received Me. There is no waiting period, no life here and another there—eternal life begins now if you choose to let it rise up and live in you."

YOUR STRENGTH AND PURPOSE

"DID YOU EVER see a ball made out of strands of straw? They are all mixed up and going in different directions, yet form a perfect ball.

This is My body. It has many different strands and not all are going in the same direction, each having a different purpose. Ultimately, it forms one body.

If all had gone in the same direction, it would never have come together. The time is coming when it will all melt together and become a force of power the world has never seen. Truth will be its strength and weaknesses will fade away. Strength will become like granite and encase the power of My Name in a way you have never known.

Do your part. Listen for My direction and then follow it—that's all you have to do. You will find that the direction you take will fill the place I have prepared for you, and in that place is your strength, power, and purpose."

USE YOUR WELL

"YOU CAN LOWER a bucket into a well, but if there is no water in the well, the bucket will come up empty.

Be careful to keep your well full—and be careful of what you fill it with.

My Word will fill your well, but My grace and the experience of My Presence will make that water like fine wine.

If you read My Word, apply My Word throughout your day, keep your eyes on Me, recognize My Presence, and both receive and give My grace to others. Your water will change to wine, your tears to joy, and your heart to abiding love."

HEALING A HURT

"A PERSON WHO is hurt carries an understanding other people don't have. Through his understanding, this person becomes a healer to those with similar circumstances.

When a knee needs to be bandaged, you don't wrap up the arm. It is the wound that needs to be wrapped. The balm or soothing medication is first the confession of the wrong. When the offender is not only sorry but <u>understands</u> the hurt he caused, the wound is on the way to healing. Love becomes the bandage that covers the wound until there is not even a scar left.

When I say, 'Confess your sins to one another,' (James 5:16 ESV) aside from seeking prayer for your faults, it means to bring healing and restoration to those you have hurt and to those who have hurt you. This will restore the wounded area completely.

This is why I ask you not only to confess your sins to Me but also to each other, so that no scars remain."

JOY IN THE ARK

"PUT YOUR TRUST in Me. When you trust, it is like being in an ark. It doesn't matter what is going on, you are safe.

You have heard that I am The Ark. But have you ever experienced that, or do you just use it as a symbol? Trust Me. Really trusting in Me will bring you peace that is truly beyond understanding. Test yourself. You will know your trust is weak if your joy is weak.

Peace comes when there are no side issues—like doubt, fear and worry. These things are what hold back My power. If you truly trust Me, there will be no room for these things. Peace will fill all the gaps in your faith. Faith is believing, and trust is resting in faith.

Be at peace and learn to recognize My hand, My presence and My leading. As you do, your peace will increase and a new ability to rest will culminate in joy.

Enter the Ark and you will enter serenity."

MAKE YOUR FLESH POWERLESS

"YOUR FLESH WORKS to weaken your inner man.

The flesh is tangible—it feels pain, it gets hungry, it gets tired, and it is the focus of the devil. His playground is your flesh, so guard it. Pour My Word into your inner man and it will feed your soul. That is why I was so careful to take time alone with My Father.

When your flesh is under attack, turn inward to your spirit and draw from Me. Your soul (mind) will be transformed as readily as you feed your spirit. Your weapon against the devil is the truth. To speak it, you have to take it in.

If the devil can get you to think his thoughts, he has usurped the life in your spirit. He will use his lies to deceive you just like he did in the garden. That is why it is so important for you to hold onto My Word—don't make excuses or even try to give the devil's thoughts credibility.

Know My Word and trust it. My greatest joy is when you live by My Word and trust that I tell you the truth."

WHAT IS YOUR WHOLE WORLD?

"WHAT IS THE whole world to you? Is it all of creation—the planets, the sun, the moon, the earth? Is it your life? Your family, your job, your dreams?

What do you think the whole world is to Me? Yes, I love My creation, but it is not My whole world—but it is FOR you.

YOU are My whole world. Just you. Just the two of us. People have taught that I would have died even just for one person and that is true. But it has become just another part of the gospel presentation and not really a personal experience.

I want you to spend the day thinking about that—just YOU and I. You are My whole world. Again, think about that and carry it with you all day. Imagine it. Pause—think. YOU and I. All day. I see you and love you. I share your life, I focus on your ups and downs and on your every moment. I share every hurt, every joy, every emotion—it all becomes Mine. It's always YOU and I.

If you ever really 'got this,' you would never lose your deep down confidence in Me. Again think about that—really think about that. You are never alone, it's always YOU and I."

GLORY IN RAIN OR SHINE

"WHEN YOU ARE down or discouraged, lift your face and let the sun smile on you. Keep your face lifted until the shadows in your heart leave.

If it is raining, lift your face and let it cleanse you from the 'puddles' of your thoughts and bring new understanding and refreshment.

Creation is filled with arms of love and carries all the comfort of My heart while soothing your wounds.

When you left the garden, I let the caress of its presence go with you to bring the power of healing. When you gaze at creation, you are gazing at My heart. It wants to enrapture you with the power and glory of My Kingdom.

The world has fallen so short and so far from what can be known and realized of My depths concerning you. You are not a superficial overflow of My being but born from the very core of Who I am.

So lift your face in rain or shine and let the glory of My universe bring healing and comfort."

DO YOU HAVE AN OCEAN WITHIN YOU?

"THERE IS AN ocean between us, and it is not of My making.

I know that to you it seems real, but you create it with your own guilt, shame, remorse, sorrow, or lack of faith. But don't forget—I can part your sea. If you decide to come to Me, the sea will open up before you.

Why do you go outside of your own house to look for what is within? Don't look at your weaknesses or your failures—I will take care of them. Look for My strength and faithfulness to keep My Word.

It is I who am at work within you. Don't give room to the devil in your mind, he loves to trick, lie, and rob you of My life. Use your authority and get him out of your house—I will light the fire of My Spirit, and truth will prove itself as we draw, in truth, together.

Why would you give your mind over to lies? Use your sword. Stand against it. Bring it to its knees. And I will raise you to new heights."

HABITS

"YOU ARE THE truck. The trailer holds all of your memories, emotional history, habits, and practices.

The truck runs easier and uses less gas when it is not pulling the trailer. So park the trailer.

Don't drag it around with you—let each day be new. See what the day brings and flow with it. It is a gift. If you pull all of your past every day, you will slow down your journey and drain your fuel.

Be open to what is new, or try doing things differently. Let life drive you. Life brings joy and makes hard things easy. You will gain more by being open to new avenues, and the pressure will leave.

Habits can be good, but they can also hinder. If you feel bored or weighed down, it is not life—change how you're doing it."

THE CHILD AND THE MOUNTAIN

A HUGE MOUNTAIN and a pebble—side by side. Almost like a mother and her baby, except the mountain was much larger in comparison. The weight of the pebble was so little that it could be tossed by a child's hand. The mountain, of course—it was immovable. I heard…

"All things are created by Me, therefore, all things are in submission to Me. Both the pebble and the mountain bow before Me. No matter your age in the spirit or the amount of your teaching, if you give your all to Me you will bring Me glory and My glory will remain in you.

'Be strong in the Lord and in the power of His might.' (Ephesians 6:10 ESV) The faith of a child, when weighed against the Pharisee, is able to move the mountain, for I am the one Who moves it.

This can only come by walking with Me—not just daily, but moment by moment. This is where your knowledge of Me grows. Keep Me at a distance and you will only know Me from a distance. Consider our oneness every step of the way. I don't come and go—'In Me, you live and move and have your being.' (Acts 17:28 NIV) That is where faith is born and grows."

THE FUNNEL

I SAW A funnel—the wide opening was up in the heavens and narrowed as it went down toward the earth. It was like the opening from heaven was so wide that lots of blessings were poured out in it and would fit in it, but as it reached the receptacle (us), the opening became very small. This is a very descriptive picture of our earthly limitations.

"Learn to focus on the large blessings—look up. Don't reduce them to fit only your momentary needs. My vision for you is much larger—not just for material blessings, which are everyone's highest focus, but for the things within you that might make you different from everyone else. I don't make duplicates. Even twins have their differences. Love, accept and discover those things in you that seem more like wishes than anything else—those things that seem too difficult or beyond your capabilities. **Remember that the top of the funnel is My will,** and it holds many blessings. Lift your eyes and receive. I have given you all that you need. Why do you continue to limit everything to your own strength? Use what is in your hand."

READING THE MENU

"WHEN YOU PRAY, pray with your heart. That's where the power is. Words can't carry any power if they are just recited without heartfelt meaning.

Better to have heartfelt prayers that only fill 10 words than a page full of emptiness that just passes through your lips.

Read the Psalms—and hear their cry. It is not to beg but to enter the presence of My Heart. Let words come from your heart, or let your heart enter the written words—but don't get trapped in recitation.

Reading and reciting with only your mind is like going to a restaurant and reading a menu but never ordering or eating the food. It all sounds good, but you will still starve.

I yearn for your love, and I yearn to express our oneness in shared hearts—for you to grow in the knowledge of our relationship. Take time to feel the ache in My Heart, to commune with you. Know that I reach out to you daily—turn to Me with a deeper and deeper desire to know Me, and you will always find Me waiting."

SEARCHING FOR INFINITY

I HAD SEEN the most amazing post on mathematics and how numbers and formulas actually take on beautiful forms and just keep multiplying into infinity. They have no end.

While I was thinking about how amazing this is, I heard…

"You see the universe and you are amazed—yet men think that they can go beyond what they see and understand. Here, they find only more and more depths—endlessly multiplying into eternity. They think they can discover the depths of My world without discovering Me. How vain.

The world is an expression of who I am. I am infinity. I have no end and no one can reach My depths.

My heart can carry it all. I can carry the world and all it contains and bring life to those who seek it. They will pass into eternity and forever enjoy its glory. I am light, I am life, I am all-powerful, and I am everywhere. I have no beginning and no end. And I am love.

My heart breaks for those who choose not to seek Me and share in the magnitude of My love—for those who choose an eternal darkness that never ends.

People keep wishing for My return. I ask you to wait with Me. Wait and pray for the return of those I love to join us in eternal life. I am anxious to come but not at the expense of losing those I created to share in My glory."

ONE TURN

"DO YOU BLAME Me? Am I the cause of your troubles? Am I the cause of your turmoil? I am the answer, not the problem. Those who blame Me simply don't know Me or don't want to know Me.

They live a life within the scope of their own understanding. They unwind the cycle of life—and cause great confusion in the spirit within them. Their spirit is as dead, denied life by the ruling mind and its own inaccuracies. The mind rules while the spirit that was given to reign is held captive, then they blame Me for all that goes wrong. And it always will go wrong because it is ruled by the flesh, and flesh cannot reign over anything but death.

They look for life in a graveyard while at the same time, they expect life with all of its blessings. When these blessings don't come, they blame Me. They may be satisfied in the flesh, but the emptiness and death within them becomes a shadow that hovers over them.

It's so sad to see—it only takes one turn to find the light that will dispel the darkness, one turn from death to life, from turmoil, to peace. One turn from the flesh to raise the spirit. One turn to Me. It's so simple. And the light and the life and the peace that will last forever, just takes one turn to Me."

KNOW YOUR AUTHORITY

"HOW DO YOU know My will? When you walk in My will, even without the mental knowledge or understanding of it, you will feel peace. But when your mind understands and cooperates, it will bring strength and confidence.

Knowing My will in a personal way gives you the assurance of authority. So conquer your fears and issues with My Word. If you don't know the Word, even though you have peace, you carry no authority. So you need My Word for, 'It is a lamp unto your feet' (Psalm 119:105 KJV) and will light your way, giving you the assurance of its fulfillment.

You can't agree with someone if you don't know what they think. The more of My Word you know, the more we will walk in agreement. So always seek your answers in My Word—you'll find peace, authority, and the confidence to carry out My purpose."

HIS STEW

"THE WORLD IS like a stew—it contains all sizes, shapes, colors, textures, and flavors all mixed together to make something delicious.

How wonderful it will be when the stew is done. When its flavors have come together and become a wonderful aroma of goodness. It has to cook long to become tender and absorb the combination of flavors. It is best to let it simmer and not let it boil, or it will become too tough to enjoy. It has to be cooked carefully and be stirred often so that the flavors will continue to mix and the stew will not get 'stuck' to the bottom of the pan. With patience, it will all come together and be a wonderful measure of blessing."

Do you see a lesson in this? Please pray for the world to see, experience and be seasoned into Gods love and pur[ose."

LIFE-CHANGING WATERS

I SAW A beautiful stream with flowers along the edge …

"This is how you draw people to My life-giving water—you draw them with the fragrance and beauty of My love. It is My heart being poured out through yours, so make room by emptying all of your negative thoughts and feelings.

To be a vessel of love, you must be able to minister from a clean heart. Don't try to minister love out of a heart that has hidden hurts, resentment, or unforgiveness.

Negative feelings can stick harder and faster than love because that is the way of the world. It is so negative and filled with sin that the natural acceptance of negativity becomes automatic.

Turn from your problems, sin or remorse. Let Me cleanse you and soak you in My love. Then you can wear on the outside what you feel on the inside. My living waters will flow freely, bringing the activity of love and depositing a life-changing anchor of faith."

THE INDESCRIBABLE
POWER OF GOD

DID YOU EVER try to fathom God—the things He has made or done? He holds the planets in place, He holds all power, all intelligence, all knowledge. He causes all things to grow, giving them sun and water to feed the whole world and meet every need. Light, life, food, energy, power, provision, and care. He has a purpose for everything He has made, everything that hangs in the universe has a purpose. He causes all things to function in whatever that purpose is. Who can imagine what it is really all about? Science tries but only discovers more and more astounding questions.

Then, out of a love we cannot comprehend, He left His Royal Throne to go to a cross and submit, ever so humbly, to all He has made. I can't comprehend this. But I can feel the thunder and the power of His resurrection when all of His creation applauded with shouts of joy, honor, and love for its Creator and Father.

I can't, as hard as I try, grasp any of these things—and I fall limp at the thought of what I cannot see.

He came to save us, yes—but also to heal His own broken heart. The heart that yearns for our presence, as much as we yearn for His.

Dear Reader,

I pray these words have blessed you and will continue to do so as your heart reaches out to Him with every need.

I am filled with a desire to impress upon you that our Lord's desire is for you to experience personally, His understanding of your being. May you receive these words directly from His Heart to yours.

So we end with a prayer that we will get past ourselves and fall easily into the love He offers. His heart is reaching out to us and His desire is for us to receive Him, knowing and accepting that we are not worthy and never will be. We will just rest freely in Him from now into eternity. God bless you.

With love,
Pam

Printed in the United States
by Baker & Taylor Publisher Services